peleliu 1944

the forgotten corner of hell

JIM MORAN & GORDON ROTTMAN

peleliu 1944

the forgotten corner of hell

Praeger Illustrated Military History Series

Westport, Connecticut
London

Library of Congress Cataloging-in-Publication Data

Moran, Jim, 1954–
    Peleliu 1944 : the forgotten corner of hell / Jim Moran and Gordon L. Rottman.
       p. cm – (Praeger illustrated military history, ISSN 1547-206X)
    Originally published: Oxford: Osprey, 2002.
    Includes bibliographical references and index.
    ISBN 0-275-98275-0 (alk. paper)
    1. Peleliu, Battle of, Palau, 1944. I Rottman, Gordon L. II. Title. III. Series.
    D767.99.P4M67   2004
    940.54'2666–dc22 2003066245

British Library Cataloguing in Publication Data is available.

First published in paperback in 2002 by Osprey Publishing Limited, Elms Court,
Chapel Way, Botley, Oxford OX2 9LP. All rights reserved.

Copyright © 2004 by Osprey Publishing Limited

Library of Congress Catalog Card Number: 2003066245
ISBN: 0-275-98275-0
ISSN: 1547-206X

Praeger Publishers, 88 Post Road West, Westport, CT 06881
An imprint of Greenwood Publishing Group, Inc.
www.praeger.com

Printed in China through World Print Ltd.

The paper used in this book complies with the Permanent Paper Standard issued
by the National Information Standards Organization (Z39.48-1984).

10 9 8 7 6 5 4 3 2 1

ILLUSTRATED BY: Howard Gerrard

CONTENTS

KEY TO MILITARY SYMBOLS

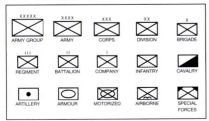

XXXXX	XXXX	XXX	XX	X
ARMY GROUP	ARMY	CORPS	DIVISION	BRIGADE
REGIMENT	BATTALION	COMPANY	INFANTRY	CAVALRY
ARTILLERY	ARMOUR	MOTORIZED	AIRBORNE	SPECIAL FORCES

INTRODUCTION

ORIGINS OF THE CAMPAIGN

By 1944 Japan was well and truly on the defensive. The glorious victories of 1941 and 1942 all across the Far East and the humiliation of the Allies were now just dim memories. In Burma, their offensive towards Imphal and Kohima had failed. By July, British and Commonwealth troops were pushing them back into central Burma.

STRATEGIC SITUATION, LATE 1944

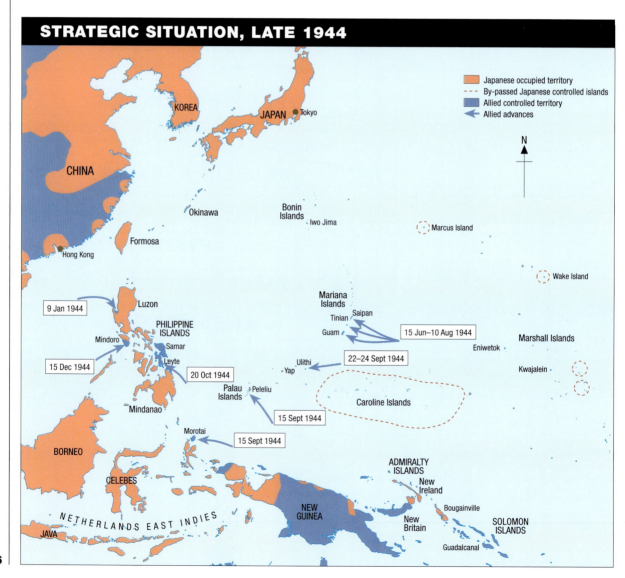

Japanese occupied territory
By-passed Japanese controlled islands
Allied controlled territory
Allied advances

President Roosevelt met with Admiral Nimitz and General MacArthur in July 1944 in Honolulu, Hawaii, to discuss Operation Stalemate, the planned assault on the Palau islands group, A target date of 8 September was set; this was subsequently revised to 15 September.

In the Northern Pacific, Admiral Chester W. Nimitz's forces had successfully "island hopped" from Tarawa in the Gilbert Islands in November of 1943, on to Kwajalein and Eniwetok in the Marshall Islands in early 1944 and to Guam, Saipan and Tinian in the Marianas, which were secured by August of 1944. Now Nimitz and his team had their sights set on Iwo Jima and Okinawa and the final objective, the Japanese Home Islands.

The delays in securing the Marianas would have two effects upon the Peleliu operations; firstly the delayed arrival of the III Amphibious Corps Commander, MajGen Roy S. Geiger, USMC, to take up his post, by which time planning for the Palau Islands operation was complete and he would have little time to change anything. Secondly, the inter-branch rivalry between the Army and the Marine Corps came to a head when LtGen Holland ("Howlin Mad") Smith, USMC, relieved MajGen Ralph C. Smith, US Army, of his command of the Army 27th Infantry Division for "defective performance." This act was to have serious repercussions all the way back to Washington, DC and the smoke from this serious bust-up was still much in evidence by the time of the Palaus operations. It must be said however that the two major players in the forthcoming operations, the 1st Marine Division (Mar. Div.) and the Army's 81st Infantry Division (Inf. Div.), would perform very well together with no repetition of what occurred on the Marianas.

In the Central Pacific, General Douglas MacArthur's forces had, since August 1942, worked their way from Guadalcanal up through the Solomons chain of New Georgia, Bougainville, New Britain, and across New Guinea. General MacArthur was now ready to fulfill his promise of "I shall return," made to the Philippine people when he was ordered to leave by President Roosevelt in the dark early days of 1942.

The successful carrier-based air strikes on the Japanese naval bases at Truk in the Caroline Islands and at Rabaul in the Solomons had neutralized them sufficiently to allow them to "wither on the vine." They were no longer a barrier to progress. MacArthur was determined to return to the Philippines as early as possible and in July of 1944 met with President Roosevelt and Admiral Nimitz in Honolulu. He argued that his failure to fulfill his pledge to return at the earliest possible moment would not only have an adverse psychological effect on the Philippines, but would also seriously diminish America's prestige amongst her friends and allies in the Far East. MacArthur was so persuasive that he even won over Admiral Nimitz, to the extent of once again securing the loan of the 1st Mar. Div. as he had done for the re-taking of the Solomon Islands. Earlier in May 1944, Admiral Nimitz had already issued a warning order for the invasion of the Palau Islands group under the codename of Operation Stalemate. The target date was set for 8 September 1944.

Initial plans were for MacArthur to push north from New Guinea to Morotai and then on to the Philippines. With the Philippines back in US hands, the decision could then be made whether to assault the Japanese mainland via Formosa and China, favored by MacArthur, or from Okinawa and the Ryukus Islands as favored by Nimitz. On the same day as MacArthur's troops landed on Morotai Island in the Netherlands East Indies between the Philippines and New Guinea, the 1st Mar. Div., supported by the 81st Inf. Div., were to make landings in the southern Palaus on the islands of Peleliu and Angaur, as part of Operation Stalemate II, the revised plan for assaulting the Palau Islands. The original plan, Operation Stalemate, had to be revised due to the delays in the Marianas campaign the troops and shipping from which constituted a large portion of the resources for Stalemate. The revised target date for Operation Stalemate II was to be 15 September 1944.

Admiral William F. "Bull" Halsey, as Commander of Western Pacific Task Force, was in overall charge of the supporting operations and, whilst the invasion force was plowing towards the Palaus, he carried out air strikes with carrier-based planes on the southern and central Philippines, as well as air strikes against the Palaus, all part of the pre-invasion preparations.

One thing was becoming apparent as a result of these air strikes; although inflicting heavy damage to enemy shipping and aircraft, the raids on the Philippines were only lightly contested. This suggested to Halsey that they were not as heavily defended as everyone had at first thought. So convinced was he that he was right, Halsey ordered his chief of staff, Rear Admiral R.B. Carney, to send an urgent message to Admiral Nimitz on 13 September, just two days before the planned assaults on Morotai and the Palaus, recommending:

1. Plans for the seizure of Morotai and the Palaus be abandoned.
2. That the ground forces earmarked for these purposes be diverted to MacArthur for his use in the Philippines.
3. That the invasion of Leyte be undertaken at the earliest possible date.

Upon receiving the urgent communiqué, Admiral Nimitz reacted quickly to Halsey's suggestions and in turn sent his own communiqué to the Joint Chiefs of Staff, who were then in Quebec for the Octagon Conference with President Roosevelt and Prime Minister Churchill. The

Admiral Chester Nimitz, as Commander-in-Chief, Pacific Fleet and Commander-in-Chief, Pacific Ocean Areas (CINCPAC – CINCPOA), was in overall command of Operation Stalemate II and it was his final decision that the invasion of Peleliu would go ahead.

Several new innovations were tried as part of the assault landing phase on Peleliu to overcome the obstacle of the coral reef, which was impassable for conventional landing craft. These included amphibious trailers towed by LVT amtracs and fully waterproofed Sherman tanks that could wade the 700 yards from the reef to the beaches. Also engineers' barges with crawler cranes were employed at the reef's edge for speedy transfer of supplies and ammunition to the beachhead by LVT amtracs.

Joint Chiefs consulted with General MacArthur and on 14 September, the day before D-Day on Peleliu, it was decided to speed up the landings on Leyte by two months – confirming point 3 of Halsey's recommendations to Nimitz. Points 1 and 2 of Halsey's recommendations were, however, ignored. This would have little effect on the 31st Inf. Div. assaulting Morotai, which cost little in blood, but for the 1st Mar. Div. and the 81st Inf. Div. this decision would cost them over 9,500 casualties.

Admiral Nimitz never fully explained his decision to overrule Halsey, saying only that the invasion forces were already at sea, that the commitment had already been made and that it was too late to call off the invasion. The Palau Islands had excellent airfields from which an invasion force against the Philippines could suffer air attacks. Also, there were several thousand first-rate troops who could be sent to reinforce the Philippine garrison. Both factors, Halsey insisted, could be dealt with by the use of air strikes and naval bombardments, without having to commit ground troops, but Nimitz overruled him.

Halsey would always disagree with Nimitz's decisions regarding Morotai and the Palaus, claiming that whatever the value of the airfields and anchorages afforded by the Palaus, the cost of taking them would be too high. A view many a soldier and marine on Peleliu would agree with.

From the Japanese perspective, the loss of the Marshall Islands and the heavy raids on Truk and the by-passed Caroline Islands necessitated serious consideration to the defense of the Home Islands. On all fronts, the Japanese were being pushed back and it was becoming apparent that a different approach would be required in the light of the pending invasion from the Allies.

The result of these serious deliberations was what became known as the "Absolute National Defense Zone." A line drawn in the sand, to be held at all costs. Part of the "National Defense Zone" was the Palau Islands. In 1944, after meetings and consultation, Premier Tojo summoned LtGen Sadao Inoue. Sadao's 14th Division had been transferred from Manchuria to the Palau Islands. There, Sadao was to prepare defenses and ready himself for the anticipated Allied invasion.

ABOVE **LtCol Nakagawa Kunio, Commander of the 2nd Infantry Regiment (Reinforced), appointed to the defense of Peleliu and Angaur. A most able tactician, as he was to prove on Peleliu, and probably ranking with General Kuribayashi, the defender of Iwo Jima, as Japan's most talented tacticians.**

TOP RIGHT **Beach Scarlet photographed after the island of Peleliu had been taken. This was one of the beaches discarded as a possible landing beach, due to the danger of troops converging on fellow assault troops advancing from Orange Beach. As can be seen from this photograph, Beach Scarlet was covered with antiboat obstacles including coconut log barriers, barbed wire entanglements, and hundreds of antiboat mines.**

The Palau Islands and the rest of the Japanese Mandated Territory (Marshall, Mariana, and Caroline Islands) had first been seized by the Japanese after declaring war on Germany in August 1914, with Admiral Tatsuo Matsumara landing on Koror in October of that year. In spite of American opposition, the League of Nations mandated control of the islands to Japan in 1920, effective in 1922. Japan established the South Sea Defense Force to secure the Mandate and it was administered by the South Sea Bureau with all commercial enterprises run by Japanese firms. Coconuts and fish were the main exports. By the early 1930s Japanese colonists far outnumbered the native population.

During the intervening years between World War I and the outbreak of World War II, Japan established a major presence on the Palaus, centered around Koror, with a civil government and a major Japanese commercial activity, but the islands always remained somewhat shrouded in secrecy. In fact it was on Koror Island that LtCol Earl (Pete) Ellis, USMC, died under mysterious circumstances in 1922 whilst "touring" the Pacific (he was in fact spying for the US Government). Ellis had argued the inevitability of a clash in the Pacific between the United States and Japan.

Japan withdrew from the League of Nations in 1935 and closed the Mandate to westerners. Japan began establishing military and naval installations throughout the Mandate, but with the exception of Truk, where a large forward naval and air base was built, most of these installations were minor. They included airfields, seaplane bases, submarine bases, and minimal coast defenses. The 4th Fleet, and amphibious force, was organized in 1939 to defend the islands.

But, following the outbreak of hostilities in December 1941, the Palau Islands took on a more important role, first as a forward supply base and training area for the Japanese conquests of 1941 and 1942, but now in 1944 they were on the front line of the defense of the homeland. Before the arrival of General Sadao and his forces, the Palau Islands were defended by troops under the command of MajGen Yamaguchi. Yamaguchi's troops would bolster Sadao's forces for the defense of the Palaus.

The Japanese, after detailed surveys, assumed correctly that the Allies would probably assault from the south, with landings on Peleliu (for the airstrip) and Angaur, then make their way up the Palaus chain, heading for Koror and Babelthuap. As events would transpire, though, this would

THE PALAU ISLANDS, 1944

English and Japanese terms
Sho — Reef
Shoto — Group of islands
Suido — Channel
To — Island

Kossol Passage
(Kosusoru Suido)

Cormoran Reef
(Korumoran Sho)

Kawasak Passage

Galap

Ngardmau

BABELTHUAP
(Baberudaobu To)

Melekeiok

Mukeru

Airfield

Goikul

Submarine
base

Arakabesan I.

Seaplane
base

Seaplane base

Madalai
(Koror Town)

KOROR
(Kororu To)

Malakal Passage

URUKTHAPEL
(Urukutaaburu To)

Yoo Passage

Ngemelis I.
(Gamirisshu Shoto)

EIL MALK
(Makarakaru To)

Ngeregong Is.

Denges Passage
(Dengisu Suido)

Garakayo Is.
(North Is.)

Ngesebus-Kongauru Is.
(Airfield under construction)

Airfield

Ngardololok

PELELIU
(Periryu To)

N

Saipan

ANGAUR
(Angauro To)

0   5 miles

0   10 km

MajGen Murai Kenjiro, sent from Koror island headquarters by General Inoue to Peleliu to add rank to Col Nakagawa, who was experiencing severe difficulties in cooperation from the naval garrison under the command of Vice Admiral Seiichi Itou. It would appear that Murai acted to all intent and purposes as an advisor to Nakagawa, not taking over command as a General should. Murai would serve on Peleliu throughout the battle at Nakagawa's side, eventually the two committing suicide.

Col Harry D. "Bucky" Harris, Commander, 5th Marines, seen here on Peleliu conferring with MajGen Roy S. Geiger, Commanding General, IIIAC (left), and William H. Rupertus, Commanding General, 1st Mar. Div. (right), prior to 5th Marines operations in northern Peleliu.

prove unnecessary to the Allies, being able to neutralize the Japanese forces on these islands with the use of air and naval supremacy from their newly acquired bases on Peleliu and Angaur.

Palau Islands

The Palau Islands, or *Parao Shoto* as the Japanese called them, are on the extreme west end of the Carolines. Yap is 350 miles to the northeast, Truk just over 1,000 miles to the east, Guam is 730 miles to the northeast, and the Philippines are 600 miles to the west. Tokyo is 2,400 miles north and Hawaii 4,600 miles east-northeast.

The Palaus contain some 100 islands and islets about 100 miles from southwest to northeast. A barrier reef runs along the west side of the islands from just northwest of Peleliu, looping out from the central islands, along the west side of Babelthuap, and around the island's north end at the Kossol Passage. The reef provides a protected lagoon suitable for a fleet anchorage. The largest island in the group is Babelthuap at 10 by 16 miles. Hilly and densely forested, its highest elevation is 794 feet. An airfield was built near the southeast end. Scores of small islands stretch from the southwest of Babelthuap. Among these are Koror Island, home of the Palaus' administrative center, naval headquarters, and a submarine base. Another submarine base and a seaplane base were on neighboring Arakabesan Island.

Peleliu Island is 25 miles southwest of Babelthuap. The Japanese called it *Periryu* and the Allied codename was "Earthenware." An extremely irregular-shaped island, Peleliu has been likened to a lobster's claw. From its northeast end to its southwest it is approximately 6 miles long and slightly over 2 miles wide in the south. That area is relatively low and flat and the Japanese built a fully developed X-shaped naval airfield there. Good landing beaches, fronted by a reef up to 1,600 yards wide, lie on the west shore. Most of the deeply indented southeast shore is lined with dense mangrove swamps, shallow bays, and a fringing reef. A few small, low islands lie offshore. A 3,500-yard long, approximately 1,000-yard wide peninsula runs to the northeast with a wide reef on the island's northwest side. In 1944 roads followed the shores on both sides of the peninsula. Low, flat, scrub tree-covered Ngesebus and Kongauru Islands lie off the end of the peninsula. Ngesebus was connected to the northeast end of the peninsula by a 600-yard timber causeway and a 100-yard causeway connected Kongauru to Ngesebus. A 60cm (24in.) narrow-gauge railroad crossed the 600-yard causeway. The Japanese were constructing an airstrip on Ngesebus. More small islands, called the Northern Islands by the Americans, were scattered to the northeast of Ngesebus and Kongauru.

The southern end of Peleliu and its eastern peninsula are low, fairly level, and mostly covered by brush and scrub trees. The beaches where the Marine landing occurred were covered with coconut palms. North of the airfield and approximately one-third the way up the northeast peninsula are the Umurbrogol Mountains. These are extremely rugged raised coral and limestone hills and ridges honeycombed with outcroppings, gorges, crags, sinkholes, and caves. Faced with cliffs up to 60ft high, they rose to 550ft above sea level. The low "mountains" were covered with dense forests and US intelligence had no idea of how chaotic the terrain was beneath them and even assessed them as being low rolling hills. The Japanese turned these craggy terrain features into fortifications and built scores of concrete pillboxes and bunkers providing interlocking fields of fire and mutual support. Virtually every cave was turned into a strongpoint and often interconnected to others by tunnels. It proved to be impossible to attack one position without coming under fire from two or more other positions. Most of the vegetation in the area was blown away during the weeks of the battle. It proved to be an attacker's nightmare and a defender's dream.

The Umurbrogol Mountains stretched part-way up the northeast peninsula and then tapered out into separate limestone ridges and hills of the Kamilianlul and Amiangal Mountains, all densely covered by forest. These too would have to be cleared, but did not pose the obstacle that the Umurbrogol Mountains did. They retained much of their vegetation through the battle although it was blasted clear in some areas.

Beside the airfield, the Japanese had built hangars, support facilities, administrative buildings, barracks, and warehouses. There was also a radio direction finder station north of the airfield and near the end of the northeast peninsula was a radio station and a phosphate processing plant – the island's main commercial value. Most of these buildings were made of reinforced concrete, but for the most part were destroyed during the battle. The peninsula had a narrow-gauge railroad system to haul phosphate.

The 81st Inf. Div.'s objective, Angaur Island, is 7 miles to the southwest of Peleliu and the southernmost of the Palaus. The Japanese called it *Angsuru* and the Allied codename was "Domestic." Angaur is $2^1/_2$ miles across north to south and $1^1/_2$ miles wide across the center. It is covered mainly by gently rolling terrain, but the northeast portion consists of extremely rugged and jagged coral outcroppings and limestone ridges up to 200ft in elevation. From this area was mined phosphate. Saipan Town and the phosphate plant were on the west central coast. An extensive narrow-gauge railroad system served the northern and central portions of the island. Much of it had been pulled up though to build fortifications. Most of the island was covered with scrub brush although the center was heavily wooded. A few small lakes and swamps were scattered about the island. There were no permanent military installations on the island other than the Japanese defenses.

So, the stage was set for one of the most controversial campaigns of the Pacific War and one of the bloodiest battles in US Marine Corps history.

A few words on pronunciation. Palau is pronounced "Pelew" and Peleliu is "Pel-la-lew." Numerous place names begin with "Ng," unique to the local native blend of Polynesian and Melanesian. Americans tended to pronounce this as a syllable, "Neg," as in "Negesbus" for Ngesebus Island, but a closer approximation is "N'y" as "N'yesbus." Umurbrogol is pronounced approximately "Um-er-bro-gol."

Col Herman H. ("hard headed") Hanneken, Commander 7th Marines. Veteran of pre-war campaigns in Haiti and Nicaragua and had served as an enlisted Marine during WW1 and in October of 1919 as a captain in the Haitan Gendarmerie, earning himself the Medal of Honor for almost single-handedly killing a Cacos guerilla leader. Hanneken had served as Chief of Staff and Assistant Division Commander, 1st Mar. Div., prior to being given command of the 7th Marines in February 1944.

CHRONOLOGY

1941

7 December Japanese bomb Pearl Harbor, Hawaii; simultaneously attacking the Philippines, Wake Island, Guam, Malaya, Thailand, Shanghai and Midway

10 December Japanese invade the Philippines and also seize Guam

1942

23 January Japanese seize New Britain and New Ireland in the Bismarck Archipelago and Bougainville in the Solomon Islands

22 February President Roosevelt orders General MacArthur out of the Philippines

11 March General MacArthur leaves Corregidor and is flown to Australia. General Jonathan Wainwright becomes the new US commander in the Philippines

18 March General MacArthur appointed commander of the Southwest Pacific Theater by President Roosevelt

24 March Admiral Chester Nimitz appointed as Commander-in-Chief Pacific Fleet and Pacific Ocean Area

6 May Japanese take Corregidor as General Wainwright unconditionally surrenders all US and Filipino forces in the Philippines

4–5 June The turning point in the Pacific War; a decisive victory for the US against Japan in the Battle of Midway as squadrons of US torpedo planes and dive bombers from USS *Enterprise*, *Hornet* and *Yorktown* attack and destroy four Japanese carriers, a cruiser, and damage another cruiser and two destroyers. The US loses *Yorktown*.

21 July Japanese land troops near Gona on New Guinea

7 August The first US amphibious landing of the Pacific War occurs as 1st Mar. Div. invades Tulagi and Guadalcanal, Solomon Islands

18 October Vice Admiral William F. Halsey named as the new commander of the South Pacific Area, in charge of the Solomons–New Guinea campaign

1943

9 February Japanese resistance on Guadalcanal ends

21 June Allies advance to New Georgia, central Solomon Islands

25 August Allies secure the New Georgia lodgment

1 November US Marines invade Bougainville, northern Solomon Islands

15 December US troops land on the Arawe Peninsula, New Britain, Bismarck Archipelago

26 December Full allied assault on New Britain as 1st Mar. Div. lands on Cape Gloucester, New Britain

Col Lewis B. "Chesty" Puller, Commander of the 1st Marines. He had served in the Caribbean, Haiti, Nicaragua and China before the war and had commanded a detachment of the famous Horse Marines in Shanghai in 1933, where he acquired an almost venomous dislike of the Japanese. He had commanded a battalion of the 7th Marines on Guadalcanal where he won his third Navy Cross. His versatility and leadership in New Britain earned him the promotion to command the 1st Marines by February 1944.

1944

1–7 February US troops capture Kwajalein and Majura Atolls, Marshall Islands

17/18 February US carrier-based planes destroy the Japanese naval base at Truk Atoll, Caroline Islands

20 February US carrier-based and land-based planes neutralize the Japanese base at Rabaul, New Britain

24 April Japanese 14th Division arrives in the Palau Islands, Col Nakagawa and 10,500 troops are sent to Peleliu plus 1,400 to Angaur

29 May Operation Stalemate ordered by Admiral Nimitz, Commander-in-Chief, Pacific Ocean Areas (CINCPOA)

11 June US Marines and Army invade Saipan

19 June The "Marianas Turkey Shoot" occurs as US carrier-based fighters shoot down 220 Japanese planes while only 20 American planes are lost

7 July Operation Stalemate II – the revised plan for the invasion of the Palau Islands – is issued

18 July Prime Minister Tojo and the War and Navy Ministers are forced to resign when the invasion of Saipan is announced in Japan

Pavuvu Island was the staging area for the 1st Mar. Div. and rest and re-fit area after their fighting in the Solomons. It took the 1st Mar. Div. several months of hard work to turn Pavuvu into a habitable place. Conditions hardly helped men, most of whom were suffering from recurring bouts of malaria and other jungle diseases and as such were far from peak fitness. Coupled with the vast numbers of replacements, including for the first time draftees rather than volunteers, the 1st Mar. Div., although in theory at 100 per cent strength, was in fact far below this in terms of combat efficiency.

19 July US Marines and Army invade Guam, Mariana Islands

24 July US Marines invade Tinian, Mariana Islands

15 August American troops complete the capture of the Mariana Islands by securing Guam

27 & 29 August 1st Mar. Div. conducts practice landings for Peleliu at Tassafaronga, Guadalcanal

4 September Peleliu Attack Group departs Guadalcanal

13 September Admiral Halsey recommends the cancellation of Operation Stalemate II, but is told it is too late to cancel the invasion of Peleliu

15 September US troops invade Morotai Island, Netherlands East Indies and Peleliu Island, Palaus Islands

17 September 81st Infantry invade Angaur Island, south of Peleliu

21 September Angaur declared secure, 81st Inf. Div. available for redeployment to Peleliu

22 September 321st Regimental Combat Team begins to relieve 1st Marines on Peleliu

15 October 81st Inf. Div. relieves 1st Mar. Div. on Peleliu

20 October US Sixth Army invades Leyte in the Philippines

23–26 October Battle of Leyte Gulf results in a decisive victory for the US Navy

27 November 81st Inf. Div. declares Peleliu secure

15 December US troops invade Mindoro in the Philippines

1945

3 January General MacArthur is placed in command of all US ground forces and Admiral Nimitz in command of all naval forces in preparation for planned assaults against Iwo Jima, Okinawa, and Japan itself

9 January US Sixth Army invades Luzon in the Philippines

19 February US Marines invade Iwo Jima

16 March US Marines secure Iwo Jima

1 April US Army and Marines invade Okinawa

22 June Japanese organized resistance ends on Okinawa

5 July Liberation of Philippines declared

14 July The first US naval bombardment of Japanese Home Islands

6 August First atomic bomb dropped on Hiroshima

9 August Second atomic bomb is dropped on Nagasaki – Emperor Hirohito and the new Prime Minister Suzuki then decide to seek an immediate peace with the Allies

2 September Formal Japanese surrender ceremony on board the USS *Missouri* in Tokyo Bay as 1,000 carrier-based planes fly overhead. President Truman declares V-J Day

1947

21 April Lt Yamaguchi and 34 men surrender on Peleliu, the last formal surrender of World War II

1954

Lone Korean laborer is last man to surrender on Peleliu

OPPOSING PLANS

THE AMERICAN PLAN – STALEMATE II

O n 29 May 1944 Admiral Chester Nimitz, as Commander-in-Chief, Pacific Fleet and Pacific Ocean Area (CINCPAC-POA), issued orders for plans to be drawn up for the invasion of the Palau Islands under the codename Operation Stalemate.

The assault would be carried out in the south by III Amphibious Corps (IIIAC) against the islands of Peleliu and Angaur. At the same time, the Army's XXIV Corps would land on the main Palaus island of Babelthuap. The target date was 8 September 1944.

Soon after operational planning had commenced, several problems became evident. The Guam invasion had fallen behind schedule and was tying up IIIAC (3rd Mar. Div., 1st Provisional Marine Brigade, and 77th Inf. Div.), which were included in Operation Stalemate. Also, much of the shipping for Stalemate was unavailable due to its continued requirements in the Marianas.

Intelligence was gathered by aerial reconnaissance photographs. Also, in June 1944 the submarine USS *Seawolf* (SS-197) carried out photographic reconnaissance of the invasion landing beaches. A further reconnaissance was carried out by the submarine USS *Burrfish* (SS-312) on Peleliu and Yap beaches. An 11-man reconnaissance group of underwater demolition team (UDT) frogmen landed on the Peleliu beaches from the *Burrfish* for closer investigation relating to water depth, location of potholes and sandbars, and obstacles. With thousands of Japanese on the island they understandably did not reconnoiter inland, and the rugged terrain of the interior would come as an unpleasant surprise to the Marines. A similar operation was carried out on the Yap invasion beaches, but this time only two of a five-man reconnaissance team made it back to the pick-up point. After several unsuccessful attempts to locate their missing comrades the remaining two men returned to the *Burrfish*.

After this incident, Admiral Nimitz banned any further missions of this type. These reconnaissance missions revealed a large Japanese garrison on Babelthuap and that the island was suitable for the construction of only a limited airstrip and facilities. Whereas on Peleliu in the south there already existed an excellent operational airfield and space on Angaur for a further airstrip and facilities. Tactically, there was no reasonable justification to invade Babelthuap at all.

The most significant intelligence information to come the Americans' way was collected on the island of Saipan after its fall in July 1944. Files of the Japanese 31st Army headquarters were captured, and along with the fortuitous capture of a Japanese intelligence officer, these files revealed, among other things, the table of organization for the

MajGen William H. Rupertus, Commanding General 1st Mar. Div. At 55 years old Rupertus was not a flamboyant officer but was well thought of by many ranking generals in the Marine Corps including the then Commandant and former Commanding Officer, 1st Mar. Div., General Archer A. Vandegrift. Rupertus, like many of his fellow 1st Mar. Div. officers, had seen overseas duty prior to World War II including command of 1st Battalion, 4th Marines in Shanghai, where he clashed several times with Japanese troops. It was during his tour of duty in China that Rupertus lost his wife, daughter and son through illness, which left him very moody with bouts of depression. Rupertus had total confidence in the ability of his 1st Mar. Div. and would insist several times during the Peleliu battle that the island would be taken "shortly" by his Marines alone. Pushing his regimental commanders to the limit and possibly beyond in the case of Chesty Puller and his 1st Marines.

Men of the 1st Mar. Div. practice boarding and debarking from DUKWs, amphibious 2½ ton trucks, used by the Marines for the first time on Peleliu. DUKWs carrying artillery and ammunition following the assault waves were destroyed because of their lack of armor.

MajGen Paul J. Mueller, US Army. Commanding General 81st Inf. Div. ("Wildcats") Mueller had been with the 81st throughout training both on mainland USA and Jungle Warfare Center on Hawaii. He was confident that although lacking the combat experience of the 1st Mar. Div., his 781st "Wildcats" were just as ready for the forthcoming invasion of Peleliu. Mueller would eventually take over command of garrisoning Peleliu and the "mopping up" operations which were to last several months after Peleliu had been declared secure.

Peleliu and Angaur garrisons. These tables indicated troop strengths on Peleliu as 10,500 and on Angaur roughly 1,400 men. As a result of the various intelligence gathering efforts, and due to the Marianas campaign running behind schedule, CINCPOA issued a second warning order on 7 July canceling Operation Stalemate and replacing it with a revised plan under the codename of Operation Stalemate II, with a revised target date of 15 September.

An unusual staff arrangement was established to plan Stalemate II. IIIAC was committed to take Guam under MajGen Geiger. The IIIAC staff would be unable to plan the Palaus operation, which it was to execute. Marine MajGen Julian Smith, designated to command the Expeditionary Troops (TF 36 – the Marine and Army landing forces), was tasked to plan the operation using his own small staff augmented by some IIIAC staff officers. This temporary planning staff was designated X-Ray Provisional Amphibious Corps. It would plan the operation and IIIAC would execute it – an awkward arrangement, but necessary in order to maintain the increasing tempo of operations. X-Ray was dissolved on 15 August 1944.

Operation Stalemate II called for IIIAC as Western Landing Force and Troops (TG 36.1) to assault the islands of Peleliu with the 1st Mar. Div. as the Peleliu Landing Force (Task Unit 36.1.1) and Angaur with the 81st Inf. Div. as Angaur Landing Force (TG 36.2) as in the original Stalemate plan. In a change to the plan, however, in floating reserve would be the 77th Inf. Div. (TG 36.3), with the 5th Mar. Div. (TG 36.4) as the area reserve, at this time based on Hawaii. D-Day was set for 15 September 1944. The second phase of Stalemate II required XXIV Corps to assault the islands of Yap and Ulithi to the northeast of the Palaus on 8 October, substituting the 96th Inf. Div. for the 77th Inf. Div. who were now in reserve for IIIAC.

To support Phases I and II, the Third Fleet (Western Pacific Task Force) split its forces. The Covering Forces and Special Groups (TF 30) were retained directly under Halsey's control. The Third Amphibious Force (TF 31) was divided into the Western Attack Force (TF 32) for

Task Force organization for the Palau Operation

CINCPAC–CINCPOA: Admiral Chester Nimitz
Western Pacific Task Forces (Third Fleet): Admiral William F. Halsey

Joint Expeditionary Force (Task Force 31) (III Amphibious Force): Vice Admiral Theodore S. Wilkinson
  Fire Support Group (Task Group 31.1): Rear Admiral Jesse B. Oldendorf
  Escort carrier Group (Task Group 31.9): Rear Admiral Ralph A. Ofstie
  Mine Sweeping Group (Task Group 31.3): Commander Wayne R. Loud
  Western Garrison Group (Task Group 31.4): Commander Charles A. MacGowan
  Western Attack Force (Task Force 32): Rear Admiral George H. Fort
    Kossol Passage Detachment (Task Group 32.9) Task Group (31.3): Commander Wayne R. Loud
    Western Landing Force (Task Group 36.1) (III Amphibious Corps): MajGen Roy S. Geiger
    Peleliu Attack Group (Task Group 32.1): Rear Admiral George H. Fort
      Peleliu Landing Force (Task Unit 36.1.1) (1st Marine Division): MajGen William H. Rupertus*
    Angaur Attack Group (Task Group 32.2): Rear Admiral William H.P. Blandy
      Angaur Landing Force (Task Unit 26.1.2) (81st Infantry Division): MajGen Paul J. Mueller*
    Western Gunfire Support Group (Task Group 32.5): Rear Admiral Jesse B. Oldendorf (Task Group 31.1)
    Western Escort Carrier Group (Task Group 32.7): Rear Admiral Ralph A. Ofstie (Task Group 31.2)
  Area Reserve Troops
    Task Group 36.3 (77th Infantry Division): MajGen Andrew D. Bruce*
    Task Group 36.4 (5th Marine Division): MajGen Keller E. Rockey*
  Expeditionary Troops (Task Force 36): MajGen Julian C. Smith

Covering Forces and Special Groups (Task Force 30) (Third Fleet): Admiral William F. Halsey
  Fleet Flagship Group (Task Group 30.1): Capt Carl F. Holden
    1 BB, 3 DD
  JASASA Group (Task Group 30.7): Capt William V. Saunders
    1 CVE, 4 DE
  Fleet Oiler and Transport Carrier Group (Task Group 30.8): Capt Jasper T. Acuff
    7 CVE, 7 DD, 15 DE, 24 AO
  Service Group (Task Group 30.9)
    2 ARG, 1 ARB & others
  Heavy Surface Striking Force (Task Force 34 – to be formed from TF 38) Vice Admiral Willis A. Lee, Jr.
    7 BB, 6 CL, 18 DD
  Light Surface Striking Force (Task Force 35 – to be formed from TF 31): Rear Admiral Walden L. Ainsworth
    4 CL, 9 DD
  Fast Carrier Force (Task Force 38 – four Task Groups and TG 30.1 sailing in company): Vice Admiral Marc A. Mitscher
    8 CV, 4 CA, 8 CVL, 7 BB, 7 CL, 3 CL(AA), 60 DD

Forward Area Central Pacific (Task Force 57): Vice Admiral John H. Hoover
  Defense forces Gilberts, Marshalls and Marianas: Vice Admiral John H. Hoover
  Shore based Air force Forward Area (Task Force 59): MajGen Willis W. Hale
  Garrison Air Forces Western Carolines
    Bombardment Aviation
    Air Defense Command Palaus
    Search and Reconnaissance Aviation
    Transport Aviation
  Western Carolines Defense and Service Forces (Task Group 57.14): Rear Admiral John W. Reeves
    Peleliu Garrison Forces (Task Unit 10.15.3): BrigGen Harold D. Campbell
    Angaur Garrison Forces (Task Unit 10.15.4) Col Ray A. Dunn

* To come under control of Task Force 36 once established ashore.

Peleliu and Angaur under Rear Admiral George H. Fort and the Eastern Attack Force (TF 33) for Yap and Ulithi under Vice Admiral Theodore S. Wilkinson (also Commander, Third Amphibious Force). TF 32 itself was split into the Peleliu Attack Group (TG 32.1) with the 1st Mar. Div. directly under Admiral Fort and the Angaur Attack Group (TG 32.2) with the 81st Inf. Div. under Rear Admiral William H.P. Blandly. The Western Fire Support Group (TG 32.7) under Rear Admiral Jesse B. Oldendorf consisted of five battleships, five heavy and three light cruisers, and 14 destroyers. Eleven escort carriers of Escort Carrier Group (TG 31.2) under Rear Admiral Ralph A. Ofstie provided close air support, combat air patrols, and antisubmarine patrols, although some were detached during the operation reducing the force to seven. The Kossol Passage Detachment (TG 32.9) would sweep the passage north of Babelthuap to establish a temporary fleet anchorage and seaplane base.

For the assault on Peleliu the planners had considered four combinations of beaches:

1. Beach Purple along the southeast coast of the island had its advantages with a narrow reef and in one area it would be possible to bring conventional landing craft right up to the beach. Unfortunately, the Japanese had also thought Beach Purple to be suitable for possible landings and their strongest defenses were in this area. Also, just a short distance inland was a dense mangrove swamp that left only a narrow strip of dry ground, ideal for defense, and so Purple Beach was ultimately rejected.

2. Beach Scarlet on the southern tip of the island was quickly discarded, mainly due to the danger of converging assault troops and casualties from friendly fire.

Beach Crimson

Murphy Island

Ngesebus Island

Kongauru Island

Beach Crimson

Akarakoro Point

Phosphate Refinery

Radio Station

Amiangal Mountain

Hill Row

Radar Hill

Carlson Island

Hill 80

Beach Amber

Ngabad Island

Garekoro

Kamilianlul Mountain

West Road

East Road

Island A

Tuckers Point

Radio Direction Finder Station

Causeway — Boat Dock

Ngardololok

Umurbrogol Mountain

Asias

Barracks

Omack

The Point

HQ and Air Base Area

Beach White 1

Beach White 2

Beach Orange 1

Beach Purple

Beach Orange 2

Beach Orange 3

N

Unnamed Islet

SE Promontory

Beach Scarlet 3

Ngarmoked Island

SW Promontory

Beach Scarlet 2

Beach Scarlet 1

	Forest
	Mangrove swamp

0   1,000 yds

0   1,000 m

3. Beach Amber along the northwest coast was where the reef was widest and the northern flank was under enfilade fire from nearby Ngesebus Island. Some 300 yards inland high ground dominated the low-lying beach and failure to take this terrain would leave the beachhead under murderous artillery fire. Beach Amber was, therefore, also rejected.

4. That left Beaches White and Orange along the western coast. These provided the opportunity for a drive straight across the island from west to east over the airfield. This was the option finally chosen as the most viable.

The initial assault called for the three regimental combat teams, the 1st, 5th, and 7th Marines, to land abreast on 2,200-yard wide beachhead, each with one of their three battalions as regimental and divisional reserve. The 1st Marines (less 1/1 in regimental reserve) would land on the left flank on White Beach 1 and 2 and push inland to a pre-determined point, then wheel left to attack the southwest end of the Umurbrogol Mountains, which extended up the northeast peninsula. The 1st Marines would then push northeast along the coastal plain and the "high ground" – as intelligence described the Umurbrogol Mountains, all the way to the northern tip of Peleliu and on to Ngesebus Island, supported by the 5th Marines on their right flank.

In the center, the 5th Marines would land two battalions; one each on Orange Beach 1 and 2. The battalion on the left would link up with the 1st Marines, the other would drive straight across the airfield to the eastern shore. The 3/5, the regimental reserve, would land at H+1 (1 hour after the initial landing), pass between the other two battalions, and then participate in the movement northwards.

The 7th Marines, on the right flank, would land two battalions in column on Beach Orange 3, with their 3rd Battalion kept as divisional reserve. The two battalions ashore were to drive across to the eastern shore on the flank of the 5th Marines, then wheel right and mop up the isolated enemy forces in a drive to the southeastern tip of the island.

The 11th Marines, reinforced with IIIAC's 3rd 155mm Howitzer and 8th 155mm Gun Battalions, would land at H+1 on Beaches Orange. The 75mm pack howitzers of 1/11 and 2/11 would provide direct fire support to 1st and 5th Marines, respectively. The 105mm howitzer-armed 3/11 would support the 7th Marines and the like-armed 4/11 would provide general support to the Division along with the two 155mm battalions. All battalions were to be in-place by H+5 and would be prepared to concentrate their fires on the southwest end of the Umurbrogol Mountains. The 8th Battalion's 155mm "Long Tom" guns would also be positioned to provide fire support to the Army on Angaur 7 miles to the southwest. However, this support was never requested.

The 81st Inf. Div. was allocated to assault the island of Angaur, but only when the assault on Peleliu was considered "well in hand." Until then the 81st would become the IIIAC Reserve. Angaur would be assaulted by two of the 81st Inf. Div.'s three RCTs, the third being detached to seize Ulithi. The date for the invasion of Angaur would be set by the 1st Mar. Div. commander, MajGen Rupertus.

Landings would be made on two of Angaur's beaches simultaneously. The 322nd RCT would land on the northern Beach Red, then they would push inland, moving south and west across the island with its left flank tying in with the other assault combat team, the 321st RCT.

Landing on the eastern Beach Blue, the 321st RCT would move inland west and south across the island, with its right flank tying in with the 322nd RCT's left. Upon securing Angaur, the 81st Inf. Div. would revert to IIIAC Reserve, initially, and then garrison Peleliu and Angaur after these islands were declared secure. The 1st Mar. Div. would return to its base on Pavuvu Island.

THE JAPANESE PLAN – DEFENSE OF THE PALAUS

With the collapse of the Japanese outer frontier, the various island garrisons took on a much greater significance as part of the new "Absolute National Defense Zone." Imperial Japanese Navy (IJN) air, service, and construction units, and guard forces were the main units providing the defense under the 30th Base Force commanded by Vice Admiral Ito Yoshioka along with Imperial Japanese Army (IJA) service and sea transport units of the 57th Line of Communications Sector Unit under MajGen Yamaguchi Takso. It was subsequently reorganized into the 53rd Independent Mixed Brigade (IMB).

With the fall of the Marshall Islands and the neutralization of Truk, combined with carrier-based air strikes on the Caroline Islands, the possibility of a US invasion of the Palau Islands seemed much more likely. Truk is in the Eastern Carolines and, with its major naval and airbase, was considered the "Pearl Harbor" of the Japanese Mandate. The 14th Division, which had been transferred from mainland China to New Guinea but re-directed to Saipan, was subsequently diverted to the Palaus, where it arrived in April 1944. The commander of the 14th Division, LtGen Inoue Sadao, established his headquarters on Koror Island and deployed units to garrison Babelthuap, Peleliu and Angaur, which he considered likely targets for invasion by the Americans. The 14th Division served as the Palau District Group while the 2nd Infantry (Reinforced) was designated the Peleliu Sector Unit. The 1st Battalion, 59th Infantry (Reinforced) served as the Angaur Sector Unit.

Operationally, the defense of the Palaus was the responsibility of the 31st Army headquartered on Truk under LtGen Obata Hideyoshi. When Saipan fell in August the command was transferred to the Southern Army in Manila, the Philippines under the command of Field Marshal Count Terauchi Hisaichi.

For the defense of Peleliu, Col Nakagawa had split the island into four defense districts. The North District was defended by the 346th Independent Infantry Battalion, 53rd IMB under the command of Maj Hikino; South District by the 3rd Battalion, 15th Infantry under Capt Chiaki; East District by the 3rd Battalion, 2nd Infantry under Capt Harada, and finally the West District defended by the 2nd Battalion, 2nd Infantry under Maj Timita. The 1st Battalion, 2nd Infantry under Capt Ichioka, the 14th Division Tank Unit and Engineer Company served as the Peleliu Sector Unit Reserve directly under Capt Sakamoto, second in command of the 2nd Infantry.

In addition there were to be support units of artillery, tanks, and engineers. The Japanese planned for both defense of the beaches as well as a defense in depth, following along the lines set out by Koror headquarters in its "Palau District Group Training for Victory" order of 11 July 1944. Here headquarters stated: "The ultimate goal of this training is to minimize our losses in the severe enemy pre-landing naval and aerial bombardment and, on the very night of the enemy landing, to take advantage of the fact that their equipment is not fully consolidated, to destroy their bridgehead at one blow." It also stated that "we must recognize the limits of naval and aerial bombardment. Every soldier and civilian employee will remain unmoved by this, must strengthen his spirits even while advancing by utilizing lulls in enemy bombardment and taking advantage of the terrain according to necessity." This Nakagawa would do to great effect, taking full advantage of the numerous coral caves and sinkholes, particularly in the area of the Umurbrogol Mountains. There were to be no mass suicidal *banzai* charges, but instead a long drawn-out battle of attrition, intended to bleed the Americans white. Peleliu would be the first occasion on which American troops encountered these tactics, but they would meet them again in the future on Iwo Jima and Okinawa.

The Americans anticipated the operations on Peleliu and Angaur would be over within one week, MajGen Rupertus declaring "It will be a short operation, a hard-fought 'quickie' that will last four days, five at the most, and may result in a considerable number of casualties. You can be sure, however that the 1st [Marine] Division will conquer Peleliu." Rupertus was right about the "considerable casualties," but the 1st Mar. Div. would not take Peleliu alone, and it would be months, not days, before Peleliu was conquered.

As for the Japanese, even though Peleliu would fall to the Americans eventually, the concept of well-prepared defenses, both on the beaches and in depth, would be proven well founded. Also, the use of coordinated counter-attacks on a small scale over a long and protracted period replaced the previous frenzied *banzai* charges, so wasteful of troops' lives. These would be far more effective in "bleeding the Americans white" and it was hoped they might buy enough time for Japan to negotiate a peace. This, unfortunately for the Japanese, would not be the case.

OPPOSING COMMANDERS

AMERICAN COMMANDERS

Although in overall command of Stalemate II, the naval commanders of Third Amphibious Force had little input in the planning of the invasion of the Palaus and released control of the tactical situation once the ground troops had landed.

Vice Admiral Theodore S. Wilkinson had, in August 1943, succeeded Admiral Richard Kelly Turner as commander of the Third Amphibious Force. He was considered an intellectual and advocate of the "hit them where they ain't," island-hopping, school of thought. His subordinate flag officers, Admirals Fort, Oldendorf, Blandy, Ainsworth, Kingman, and Ofstie, all had past Pacific combat experience involving close liaison with Marine and Army units and, although there is evidence of friction previously between the Navy, Marine, and Army bodies, there does not appear to be any evidence that such friction existed between the units involved in Stalemate II.

Major General Julian C. Smith, USMC – Commanding General, Third Fleet Expeditionary Troops (TF 36). Probably most associated with the Tarawa operation, where he commanded the 2nd Marine Division. A recognized expert in amphibious warfare, Julian Smith found his new position very difficult. He felt he had little authority, being under the watchful eyes of senior officers from both the Navy and Marine Corps. Clearly, he considered his role to be overseeing

Prior to the landing of the Regimental Combat teams on beaches White and Orange, LCIs equipped with multiple rocket launchers saturate the beaches with salvos of high explosive. They then retired to join the other fire support vessels further offshore.

administrative, logistical, and tactical units – as he put it, "I filed papers." He was given responsibility for planning Stalemate II, while General Roy S. Geiger, commanding IIIAC, was still battling away on Guam. Smith had joined the Corps in 1909 to serve in Latin America, commanded the 1st Marine Brigade, and held numerous senior instructor assignments. He commanded the 2d Mar. Div. at Tarawa and was given the assignment of planning Stalemate II along with command of the Third Fleet Expeditionary Troops for the operation.

Although temporarily in charge of the planning for Stalemate II, Julian Smith still had all his regular duties to perform as Commander, Expeditionary Troops, Third Fleet, and as such did not always have the time to monitor the progress of the planning for the forthcoming assault in as much detail as he would have liked. One such detail was that the Commanding General of the 1st Mar. Div., MajGen Rupertus, had broken his ankle during landing practice on Guadalcanal. Had he known this earlier, Julian Smith would have relieved Rupertus of his command of the 1st Mar. Div., but it was too late to implement such an order by the time Julian Smith found out.

Major General Roy S. Geiger, **USMC** – Commanding General, III Amphibious Corps. MajGen Roy Geiger was almost 60 years old and his Marine Corps career had been mainly in aviation since joining the Corps in 1909. He had commanded aviation units in both World Wars, including the 1st Marine Aircraft Wing on Guadalcanal. In 1943, Geiger was appointed Director of Marine Corps Aviation, but then returned to the Pacific as Commanding General, I Marine Amphibious Corps. Considered by some to be an unusual move, placing an aviator in command of an amphibious corps, Geiger was a good choice being an expert in fire support and logistics. The I Marine Amphibious Corps was redesignated IIIAC on 15 April 1944.

Major General William H. Rupertus, **USMC** – Commanding General, 1st Marine Division. In command of the assault troops on Peleliu, at 55 years old Rupertus was not a flamboyant officer but was a good friend of Generals Holland Smith and Julian Smith and of General Vandegrift, former Commanding General, 1st Mar. Div. When Vandegrift was promoted to Commandant of the Marine Corps, Rupertus was the obvious choice to succeed him as commander of the 1st Marine Division. Rupertus, like his fellow 1st Mar. Div. officers, had seen his share of overseas duty before World War II including Latin America and China. It was during this tour of duty in China that Rupertus lost his wife, daughter, and son to an epidemic. This had a profound effect on him personally and left him very moody and with bouts of depression, which had a serious effect on his relationships with subordinates, this would become apparent during the battle for Peleliu. He was the assistant commander of the 1st Mar. Div. on Guadalcanal.

One other major characteristic of MajGen Rupertus was his obvious mistrust of the Army, not uncommon in the Marine Corps. This was mainly as a result of the differences between the Marines' and the Army's approaches to conducting battles. Rupertus did not consider it necessary to have the 81st Inf. Div. as reserve to his 1st Mar. Div. and had no intention whatsoever of calling upon their assistance in the forthcoming campaign on Peleliu.

Brigadier General Oliver P. Smith, USMC was the Assistant Division Commander. He had served as a battalion commander on Guadalcanal and was a regimental commander on New Britain. The Division Chief of Staff was Colonel John T. Selden.

At regimental level, it is probably difficult to find a more distinguished group of commanders in the US Marine Corps.

Colonel Lewis B. "Chesty" Puller, USMC – Commander, 1st Marines. Puller was a Virginian who had entered the Corps in his teens and had served with great distinction in most of the Marine Corps' "Banana Wars" of pre-World War II, serving in the Caribbean, Haiti, and Nicaragua. He had also served in China before the war and had commanded the "Horse Marines" in Shanghai in 1933, where he gained a reputation as a no-nonsense commander and brought to the fore his great dislike of the Japanese.

Chesty Puller's idea of a commander was one who leads from the front and by 1944 his leadership had become legendary. His command of the 1st Battalion, 7th Marines, as a Lieutenant Colonel, on Guadalcanal, won him his third Navy Cross. His leadership and versatility in a number of different roles on New Britain earned him promotion to the command of the 1st Marines in February 1944.

Colonel Herman H. "Hard Headed" Hanneken, USMC, Commander, 7th Marines, was like Puller a veteran of the pre-World War II Haitian and Nicaraguan campaigns. In October of 1919, as an enlisted Marine with the temporary rank of captain in the Haitian Gendarmerie, Hanneken (along with one other Marine) had infiltrated the rebel Caco headquarters and killed the rebel leader Charlemagne Peratte. This action earned him the Medal of Honor. Hanneken was to repeat, almost identically, this feat in Nicaragua ten years later by capturing Manuel Jiron, one of Cesar Sandino's top lieutenants.

Hanneken had commanded a battalion on Guadalcanal and was Chief of Staff to the Assistant Divisional Commander before being given command of the 7th Marines in February 1944. Oldest of the three regimental commanders, Hanneken was one of the "Old Corps" Marines. He never smiled, but his dedication to duty, loyalty and personal courage earned him great respect both from his men and from his fellow officers, and a well-earned reputation as a tough and fearless commander.

Colonel Harold "Bucky" D. Harris, USMC – Commander, 5th Marines. Youngest of the three regimental commanders Harris, unlike Puller and Hanneken, had not been an enlisted Marine, but was a career officer. Commissioned after graduating from Annapolis in 1925, Harris attended Army Infantry School at Fort Benning, then becoming one of the few Americans to attend the École Supérieure de Guerre in Paris, France. Harris served in various posts in the United States and saw overseas duty in China and Nicaragua. At the outbreak of World War II, Harris was stationed in Washington, DC in the Marine Intelligence Section. In 1942 he was transferred as Intelligence Officer on the staff of Commander, Amphibious Forces, South Pacific. In 1943 Harris was briefly Chief of Staff, Marine Forces Solomons, before assignment to the 1st Mar. Div. as Executive Officer, 1st Marines.

Harris served with the 1st Marines through the New Britain campaign before being appointed Division Assistant Chief of Staff, Intelligence in 1944. He was given command of the 5th Marines just prior to the invasion of Peleliu. Although Harris was new to the 5th Marines and to commanding troops in combat, the regiment would perform extremely well under his command.

Colonel William H. Harrison, USMC, commanded the 11th Marines along with attached artillery units.

Major General Paul J. Mueller, US Army – Commanding General, 81st Infantry Division. General Mueller was a very able commander who had seen his division through many months of training, both in the States and at the Jungle Warfare Center on Hawaii. He had fought as a battalion commander in World War I and held numerous staff assignments between the wars. Mueller was confident that although lacking in combat experience, his 81st "Wildcats" were just as ready for the forthcoming assault on Peleliu as the 1st Marine Division.

The Assistant Division Commander was Brigadier General Marcus B. Bell, the Commander, 81st Division Artillery was Brigadier General Rex W. Beasley, and the Chief of Staff was Colonel James C. Short.

Under MajGen Mueller for the assault on Angaur and Ulithi were three RCTs: the 321st RCT under the command of Colonel Robert F. Dark, 322nd under the command of Colonel Benjamin W. Venable, and 323rd RCT under the command of Colonel Arthur P. Watson. Like most of the men of the 81st Inf. Div., they had seen little in the way of combat, but all were professional soldiers, dedicated officers, and well trained. All would perform well in the forthcoming campaign, both in combat and in liaising with Navy and Marine units.

JAPANESE COMMANDERS

Lieutenant-General Inoue Sadao, Imperial Japanese Army, Commander, 14th Division (usually listed as Sadao Inoue or Sadai Inoue), was Prime Minister Tojo's instant choice to command the 12,000 reinforcements headed for the Palaus and to take command of all the Japanese forces, both Navy and Army, on the islands and he doubled as Commander, Palau District Group.

LVT(A)4s plough towards the Peleliu landing beaches on D-day. The massive naval and aerial bombardment continues. Admiral Oldendorf claimed to have run out of targets for his pre-invasion bombardment and sent numerous vessels on to the Philippines. His opinion of the effects of his bombardment proved sadly exaggerated.

Sadao looked like the typical Hollywood version of a Japanese officer. At the time of the battle, he was in his mid-fifties, of medium build, balding, myopic; a stern-voiced and strict disciplinarian. He was fiercely dedicated to his heritage of five generations of ancestors, all of whom had been military officers.

During the Russo-Japanese War, Sadao, as a 20-year-old sub-lieutenant, had been decorated for valor and had risen steadily through the ranks to his present position of commander of the 14th Division. Premier Tojo considered Sadao to be thoroughly competent and most suited to command such a mixed array of troops as was the Palaus garrison. What Sadao lacked in flair, he made up for with tenacity, a leader who would not crumble under adverse circumstances.

Sadao would be the only one of the senior Japanese commanders involved with the battle of Peleliu to survive the war, being tried on Guam for war crimes in China. He was found guilty and served 10 years in a US Navy prison on Guam, where he was interviewed extensively by the US military about the battle for Peleliu.

Prior to Sadao's arrival in the Palaus, the defense of the Palaus had been under the command of **Vice-Admiral Ito Yoshioka**. Upon his arrival on Koror, where he established his headquarters, General Sadao appointed Colonel Nakagawa Kunio as Peleliu's new commander, with his 2nd Infantry (Reinforced).

Colonel Nakagawa Kunio, Imperial Japanese Army, Commander, 2nd Infantry and Peleliu Sector Unit, was a most able commander, possibly one of Japan's finest defensive tacticians, in the same league as Kuribiashi on Iwo Jima. Nakagawa would make full use of all his defenses and troops on Peleliu, making the Americans pay dearly for every inch, as he had been ordered to do.

27

The Mystery of Imperial Japanese Navy command on Peleliu

Most references state that Vice-Admiral Seiichi Itou (his correct name is Ito Seiichi) was the naval commander on Peleliu and/or the Palaus and that MajGen Murai Kenjiro of the 14th Division was sent to the island to act as liaison with the naval commander, who outranked Col Nakagawa Kunio commanding Peleliu's defense. It is reported that there was conflict between the IJA and IJN on Peleliu. Ito Seiichi's photo is provided in many of these references. In reality Vice-Admiral Ito Seiichi ("Seiichi Itou") was the Vice Naval Chief of Staff and was in Japan. He took command of the 2nd Fleet in November 1944. In command of the battleship *Yamato*'s suicide mission to beach itself on Okinawa in April 1945, he went down with the ship. Vice-Admiral Ito Yoshioka (sometimes spelled "Itou" resulting in confusion; he is also listed as Ito Kenzo) commanded the 30th Base Force headquartered at Koror. It is not known if he was actually on Peleliu at any time during the battle. His headquarters was on Koror and he survived the war to surrender IJN forces in the Palaus to the Marines in 1945. No source can be found naming the senior IJN commander on Peleliu other than a single reference to a "Colonel" Oya, of the "West Carolines Air Force;" there were no "colonels" in the IJN air service although he may have been an IJN captain equivalent to a colonel. A detachment of the 45th Guard Force was on Peleliu. The force was commanded by Captain Mori Kanahisa, but his headquarters was also on Koror.

This then raises again the old question as to why MajGen Murai was on Peleliu when Col Nakagawa was in command of the defense. Lieutenant-General Sadao, when interviewed in captivity after the war, stated he was the tactical advisor and that while trusting Nakagawa, he assigned Murai there for "insurance," and to cope with the IJN under Vice-Admiral Ito, however, an IJN vice-admiral outranks an IJA major-general – a rank equivalent to a US brigadier general. In all probability Vice-Admiral Ito was not on Peleliu, but on Koror at his headquarters.

Although a very capable commander, the appointment of an Army colonel over a Navy vice-admiral caused a great rift between the Army and Navy on Peleliu, which deteriorated into farce. To resolve matters and calm the Navy down somewhat, General Sadao sent **Major-General Murai Kenjiro** from his headquarters on Koror Island to Peleliu to provide the Army with sufficient rank to satisfy the vice-admiral's honor, although the defense of Peleliu seems, to practical purposes, to have remained in the hands of Col Nakagawa. Unfortunately, both Nakagawa and Murai died in the defense of Peleliu so we will never be 100 per cent certain just who was in command of the Japanese forces.

Sent from Koror to Peleliu by General Sadao, it appears that Murai, after inspecting Nakagawa's defensive works and battle plans for the defense of Peleliu, was content to let Nakagawa continue without interference from himself, lending only the weight of his rank to acquire the required cooperation of the Navy elements on Peleliu. MajGen Murai would remain on Peleliu for the duration of the battle, fighting alongside Col Nakagawa to the bitter end, and would commit suicide along with Nakagawa in the final days of the fighting for the Umurbrogol Pocket.

As for the remainder of the Japanese officers, under the command of Col Nakagawa and MajGen Murai during the defense of Peleliu and Angaur, little is known of them other than their names and ranks, although it must be said that all of them conducted a very skilful defense obeying orders and following the new defense concept well, even though by the closing stages of the battle food, water, and ammunition were all but gone and the only communications were with Nakagawa's headquarters and General Sadao on Koror. Nakagawa's last message to Sadao summed up the position of the defenders of Peleliu, stating:

"It would be difficult to hold any position more than a day." His military forces had been reduced "to 50 unwounded and 70 wounded soldiers. They have only rifles and 20 rounds of ammunition per man and a few hand grenades."

There is evidence suggesting a rift between MajGen Murai and Col Nakagawa towards the end of the battle for Peleliu. Major-General Murai wanted to gather all remaining forces for a final glorious charge on the airfield whilst Nakagawa would have none of it, insisting upon sticking to the defense plan of remaining in defensive positions and resisting for as long as possible. These two conflicting views were reported to General Sadao on Koror. Sadao agreed with Nakagawa, communicating to Murai "it is easy to die but difficult to live on. We must select the difficult course and continue to fight because of the influence on the morale of the Japanese people. Saipan was lost in a very short time because of vain *banzai* attacks with the result that the people at home suffered a drop in morale." Major-General Murai accepted Sadao's counsel, no *banzai* charge occurred; instead he continued the defensive fight to the end, alongside Nakagawa.

OPPOSING FORCES

AMERICAN FORCES – JOINT EXPEDITIONARY FORCE

For Operation Stalemate II the Americans had assembled an impressive force as part of the Third Fleet expeditionary troops under the command of MajGen Julian C. Smith. Direct command of Western Task Force (Southern Palaus) was exercised by III Amphibious Corps under MajGen Roy S. Geiger. Both Smith and Geiger were aboard the amphibious command ship USS *Mount McKinley* (AGC-7). Main assault troops for IIIAC consisted of the 1st Mar. Div. (Reinforced) and the 81st Infantry Division.

Pre-invasion bombardment would be provided by the 14in. guns of the battleships USS *Pennsylvania* (BB-38), *Maryland* (BB-46), *Mississippi* (BB-41), *Tennessee* (BB-43), and *Idaho* (BB-42), the heavy cruisers USS *Columbus* (CA-74), *Indianapolis* (CA-35), *Louisville* (CA-28), *Minneapolis* (CA-36), and *Portland* (CA-33), and the light cruisers USS *Cleveland* (CL-55), *Denver* (CL-58), and *Honolulu* (CL-48), all supported by planes from three fleet carriers, five light carriers, and 11 escort carriers. This "softening up" of Peleliu was to commence on D–3 (12 September 1944) and continue up to and including D-Day (15 September 1944). Nevertheless, Admiral Oldendorf declared on D–1 (14 September) that he had "run out of targets" and aborted his bombardment, sending the majority of naval support ships to the Philippines to support the forthcoming landings there.

There were two elements to Stalemate II assault on the Palau Islands. First was the island of Peleliu which was to be assaulted by 1st Mar. Div. (Reinforced). Second was to be the assault on Angaur Island, to the southwest of Peleliu; this was the target of the 81st Infantry Division.

The 1st Mar. Div. had been raised in February 1941 from the 1st Marine Brigade at Guantánamo Bay, Cuba. It had fought on Guadalcanal, America's first amphibious landing in World War II, from August to December 1942. The "Old Breed" then secured a lodgment on Cape Gloucester, New Britain, fighting there from December 1943 to February 1944. To avoid being over-tasked with work details and guard duty at the new base on Guadalcanal, the 1st Mar. Div. established camp on Pavuvu Island in the Russell Islands, a small,

This view of the beaches, as seen from a Navy spotter plane, shows dozens of amtracs on or approaching beaches White 1 and 2, targets of 1/1 and 3/1 on the extreme left, just inland was "The Point," uncharted high ground bristling with Japanese defense positions, which held up 3/1 for most of D-Day, finally taken after many casualties by George Hunt's K/3/1.

inhospitable island 35 miles northeast of Guadalcanal. Rotting coconuts, rats, crabs, heat, humidity, rain, mud, and inadequate training areas made it a miserable experience for the Marines. They would reluctantly return there after Peleliu to prepare for Okinawa.

Many of the Division's Guadalcanal veterans had rotated back to the States, but some were still present and most of the troops had fought on New Britain. These men were in less than ideal condition having endured one of the wettest campaigns of the war. Most were suffering from weight loss and fungus infections, but would recover by the time of the Peleliu attack. The Division had received 4,860 replacements by June. Some 80 per cent of the Division was aged between 18 and 25.

While on Pavuvu the 1st Mar. Div. reorganized under the May 1944 tables of organization. This saw the detachment of the 1st Amphibian Tractor Battalion to Fleet Marine Force (FMF) control, but it remained attached to the Division, and the deactivation of the 1st Special Weapons Battalion with its antitank weapons reassigned to the infantry regiments. Company D (Scout) was detached from the 1st Tank Battalion, redesignated 1st Reconnaissance Company, and reassigned to Headquarters Battalion, 1st Mar. Div. At the same time "Light" was dropped from the tank battalion's designation and it received 75mm gun-armed M4A2 Sherman medium tanks to replace its M3A1 light tanks although its Company A had had Shermans since late 1943. The tank companies underwent reorganization too. Rather than three five-tank platoons as previously assigned, the medium companies had four three-tank platoons plus three in the company headquarters. This allowed for more flexible attachment of platoons to infantry battalions, but with too few tanks per platoon. A single combat loss or malfunction reduced the platoon to a relatively ineffective two tanks.

To support the assault the Division was directed to form the 3d Armored Amphibian Tractor and 6th Amphibian Tractor Battalions (Provisional) by splitting the 1st Amphibian Tractor Battalion three ways. The three battalions were manned by personnel drawn from the rear echelons of other amtrac battalions, directly from the Tracked

Support waves huddle down in Higgins boats awaiting their turn to transfer to amtracs for the trip into the beaches on D-Day. The tension is all too apparent on the faces of veteran and green replacement alike.

Vehicle School in the States, and Company C, 1st Motor Transport Battalion. Few LVTs were available to train the three units, but sufficient LVT(2)s and new LVT(4)s had arrived in time to take part in the assault. The 3d Armored Amtrac Battalion had mostly new 75mm howitzer-armed LVT(A)4s and a few old 37mm gun-armed LVT(A)1s.

The 1st Motor Transport Battalion landed with only Company A's full complement of trucks and repair equipment as the need for trucks on the small island was deemed limited, and two amtrac battalions would haul cargo. The battalion's Company B landed as litter bearers and relief drivers and Company C had been absorbed into the new amtrac units. The tanks of 1st Tank Battalion's Company C did not deploy because of limited shipping space, but the crews were brought to serve as replacements. Only 30 tanks were initially deployed, but replacements were delivered as 40 were knocked out in the fight. About 20 tanks were kept operational through the battle and of those knocked out only nine were totally destroyed.

The 17th Marines, the divisional engineer regiment, was deactivated with the engineer and pioneer battalions remaining under division-control and the naval construction battalion ("Seabees") returned to the Navy. In May the 105mm howitzer-armed 3d Battalion, 11th Marines was rearmed and redesignated the 3d 155mm Artillery Battalion and reassigned to FMF. The 5th Battalion, 11th Marines was redesignated the new 3/11. Under the new table of organization 1/11 and 2/11 had 75mm M1A1 pack howitzers and 3/11 and 4/11 had 105mm M2A1 howitzers. Artillery batteries, regardless of caliber, had four pieces.

The three infantry regiments too were reorganized. The regiments were authorized 3,236 men with a 261-man headquarters and service

company (it lost its scout and sniper platoon), 203-man regimental weapons company, and three 954-man infantry battalions. The weapons company had a platoon of four 75mm M3A1 halftrack-mounted guns and three platoons each with four 37mm M3A1 AT guns. The infantry battalions lost their weapons companies (D, H, M). The mortar platoon with four 81mm M1 mortars was reassigned to the 213-man headquarters company. The three heavy machine gun platoons were absorbed into the new rifle company machine gun platoons. Pooled in the battalion headquarters were 27 M1A1 flamethrowers and 27 demolition kits – one of each per rifle squad. Rifle companies often formed assault sections, intended to attack pillboxes, equipped with these weapons and with bazookas. For Peleliu the 1st Mar. Div. was provided 100 60mm T20 shoulder-fired mortars, supplied to rifle platoons for use as direct fire weapons against pillboxes and caves.

The 240-man rifle companies[1] had a 53-man headquarters, three 46-man rifle platoons, and a 56-man machine gun platoon. The former company weapons platoon was converted to a machine gun platoon with six .30cal. M1919A4 aircooled light machine guns and a reserve of six .30cal. M1917A1 watercooled heavy machine guns. The latter could be substituted for the light machine guns. The mortar section with three 60mm M2 mortars was reassigned to the company headquarters. There were three 2.36in. M1A1 rocket launchers in the company headquarters to be allocated as necessary along with bazookas from other battalion elements that were sometimes loaned to platoons.

The rifle platoons had a seven-man headquarters and three 13-man rifle squads organized under a new concept, although the practice went back to the "Banana Wars." It had a squad leader (M1 carbine) and three four-man fire teams, each with a fire team leader (M1 rifle, M7 grenade launcher), rifleman (M1 rifle, M7 grenade launcher), automatic rifleman (M1918A2 Browning automatic rifle – BAR), and an assistant automatic rifleman (M1 carbine, M8 grenade launcher). This gave the squad three fire-and-maneuver teams, each under a designated

Assault waves huddle down for what little protection they can find on the beaches on D-Day. Several DUKWs and amtracs can be seen burning in the lagoon in the background. 3/1 and 3/7 on the flanks of the landings suffered losses from the heavy anti-boat fire on the way in.

1 1st Bn, A–C, 2nd Bn, E–G, 3rd Bn, I, K, L; they were not re-lettered when the weapons companies were disbanded; neither the Marines nor the Army used a Company J.

1st Marine Division Organization

Combat Team 1 (Beaches White 1 and 2)
- 1st Marines
- Company A, 1st Engineer Battalion
- Company A, 1st Medical Battalion
- Company A, 1st Pioneer Battalion
- Company A, 1st Tank Battalion
- 1st Platoon, 1st MP Company
- 1st Platoon, Ordnance Company, 1st Service Battalion
- Detachment, Service and Supply Company, 1st Service Battalion
- Detachment, 4th Joint Assault Signal Company

Combat Team 5 (Beaches Orange 1 and 2)
- 5th Marines
- Company B, 1st Engineer Battalion
- Company B, 1st Medical Battalion
- Company B, 1st Pioneer Battalion
- Company B (– 1st and 4th Platoons), 1st Tank Battalion
- 2nd Platoon, 1st MP Company
- 2nd Platoon, Ordnance Company, 1st Service Battalion
- Detachment, Service and Supply Company, 1st Service Battalion
- Detachment, 4th Joint Assault Signal Company

Combat Team 7 (Beach Orange 3)
- 7th Marines (– 2nd Battalion)
- Company C (– 2nd Platoon), 1st Engineer Battalion

- Company C, 1st Medical Battalion
- Company C, 1st Pioneer Battalion
- 1st and 4th Platoons, Company B, 1st Tank Battalion
- 3rd Platoon, 1st MP Company
- Detachment, 4th Joint Assault Signal Company

Armored Amphibian Tractor Group
- 3rd Armored Amphibian Tractor Battalion (Provisional)
- US Navy Flamethrower Detachment (– one LVT to each CT)

Amphibian Transport Group
- 1st Amphibian Tractor Battalion (120 x LVT(2) & LVT(4))
- 6th Amphibian Tractor Battalion (Provisional) (80 x LVT(4))
- Detachment, 8th Amphibian Tractor Battalion (21 x LVT(2))
- 454th Transportation Corps Amphibious Truck Company (50 x DUKW) (USA)
- 456th Transportation Corps Amphibious Truck Company (50 x DUKW) (USA)

Artillery Group
- 11th Marines (1st–4th Battalions)
- 3d 155mm Howitzer Battalion
- 8th 155mm Gun Battalion (– Battery C)

Antiaircraft Group
- 12th Antiaircraft Artillery Battalion (90/40/20mm)

Engineer Group
- 1st Engineer Battalion (– Companies A-C)
- 33rd Naval Construction Battalion (–)
- 73rd Naval Construction Battalion (–)

Shore Party Group
- 1st Pioneer Battalion (– Companies A-C)
- 1st Motor Transport Battalion (– Company C)
- Detachments, 33rd and 77th Naval Construction Battalions

Service Group
- 1st Service Battalion (– detachments)
- 16th Field Depot
- 7th Marine Ammunition Company
- 11th Marine Depot Company

Medical Group
- 1st Medical Battalion (– Companies A-C; – detachment, Company D)

Reserve Group
- 2nd Battalion, 7th Marines
- 1st Tank Battalion (– Companies A-C)
- 1st Reconnaissance Company
- 2nd Platoon, Company C, 1st Engineer Battalion
- Detachment, Company D, 1st Medical Battalion

Attachments
- 4th-6th Marine War Dog Platoons
- 5th and 6th Separate Wire Platoons

leader. The Division was dissatisfied with the M1 carbine's limited stopping power and penetration through vegetation. Most carbine-equipped infantrymen were issued M1 rifles and 2/7 received both M1 rifles and M1 Thompson submachine guns to replace carbines.

The 1st Mar. Div. would comprise three infantry combat teams, plus eight task-organized support groups formed from divisional and attached IIIAC combat support and service units. The three infantry regiments consisted of the 1st Marines the 5th Marines, and the 7th Marines (Marine regiments are always designated as "Marines" and "regiment" is never included in their official designation nor is "infantry" or "artillery."). These were designated Combat Teams (CT) 1, 5, and 7 – codenamed "Spitfire," "Lone Wolf," and "Mustang," respectively. The CTs were usually augmented with tank, engineer, pioneer, and medical companies plus service detachments and a detachment from the 4th Joint Assault Signal Company to control field artillery, naval gunfire, and close air support. The 1st Pioneer Battalion had two provisional replacement companies attached. Designated Companies D and E, they unloaded landing ships until sent forward as replacements on D+3, but their numbers were inadequate. The US Navy Flamethrower Detachment, a test unit, was commanded by a Navy officer, but manned by Marines. It had six LVT(4) amtracs mounting Ronson Mk I flamethrowers with one amtrac attached to each CT and three in reserve. Army amphibious truck companies, with DUKW $2^1/_2$-ton amphibians or "Ducks," were attached to the Marines as their own operational companies were tied up in the Marianas. Ducks were mainly used to haul light artillery and ammunition ashore.

The organization of the 1st Mar. Div. (Reinforced) for the Peleliu assault is shown above.

IIIAC Reserve was to be the 81st Inf. Div. – less the 323rd RCT, which was to assault Ulithi Atoll. The remaining two RCTs, 321st and

81st Infantry Division Organization

321st Regimental Combat Team (Beach Blue – Angaur)

321st Infantry Regiment

316th Field Artillery Battalion (105mm Howitzer)

Company A, 306th Engineer Combat Battalion (+ Detachment, H&S Company)

Company A plus Company D (– 2nd Platoon) and HQ 306 Medical Battalion (– detachment)

Detachment, 781st Ordnance Light Maintenance Company

Detachment, Traffic Squad, 81st MP Platoon

Detachment, 81st Quartermaster Company

154th Engineer Combat Battalion (+ detachment, HQ & HQ Company, 1138th Engineer Combat Group)

Detachment, 592d Joint Assault Signal Company

Detachment, 481st Transportation Corps Amphibious Truck Company (DUKW)

Company A, 726th Amphibian Tractor Battalion (+ Detachment H&S Company)

Half Company D, 776th Amphibian Tank Battalion

Company A, 710th Tank Battalion

Detachment, Provisional Quartermaster Graves Registration Company, 81st Inf. Div.

Detachment, Translator-Interpreter Team A, HQ Company, Central Pacific Area

322nd Regimental Combat Team (Beach Red – Angaur)

322d Infantry Regiment

317th Field Artillery Battalion (105mm Howitzer)

Company B, 306th Engineer Battalion (+ detachment, H&S Company)

Company B, 306th Medical Battalion

Detachment, 781st Ordnance Light Maintenance Company

Detachment, Traffic Squad, 81st MP Platoon

52d Engineer Combat Battalion (+ detachment, HQ & HQ Company, 1138th Engineer Combat Group)

Detachment, 592d Joint Assault Signal Company

Company B, 710th Tank Battalion

Company D, 88th Chemical Battalion (Motorized) (4.2in. mortar)

726th Amphibian Tractor Battalion (– Company A & detachment, H&S Company)

Company D, 776th Amphibian Tank Battalion (– half of company)

Detachment, 481st Transportation Corps Amphibious Truck Company (DUKW)

Detachment, Translator-Interpreter Team A, HQ Company, Central Pacific Area

Detachment, Provisional Quartermaster Graves Registration Company, 81st Inf. Div.

17th Medical Field Hospital (– one platoon)

323rd Regimental Combat Team (Ulithi Atoll)

323d Infantry Regiment

906th Field Artillery Battalion (105mm Howitzer)

Company C, 306th Engineer Battalion (+ detachment, H&S Company) [2]

Company C, 306th Medical Battalion (+ 2d Platoon, Company D and detachment, HQ)

Detachment, 781st Ordnance Light Maintenance Company

Detachment, Traffic Squad, 81st MP Platoon

[2] Elements remaining on Angaur and did not accompany the RCT to Ulithi.

Detachment, 81st Quartermaster Company [2]

Detachment, 481st Transportation Corps Amphibious Truck Company (DUKW)

Detachment, 592d Joint Assault Signal Company

155th Engineer Combat Battalion (+ detachment, HQ & HQ Company, 1138th Engineer Combat Group)

Detachment, Provisional Quartermaster Graves Registration Company, 81st Inf. Div.

Detachment, Translator-Interpreter Team A, HQ Company, Central Pacific Area

81st Infantry Division Artillery (– three 105mm battalions)

HQ & HQ Battery, 81st Infantry Division Artillery

318th Field Artillery Battalion (155mm Howitzer)

Division Troops

HQ, 81st Infantry Division

HQ Company, 81st Infantry Division

306th Engineer Combat Battalion (– Companies A–C and detachments, H&S Company)

306th Medical Battalion (– Companies A–D and detachments, HQ Detachment)

81st Cavalry Reconnaissance Troop

Division Special Troops

HQ, Special Troops, 81st Infantry Division

81st Infantry Division Band

81st Signal Company

781st Ordnance Light Maintenance Company (– three detachments)

81st Quartermaster Company (– two detachments)

81st MP Platoon (– three detachments)

81st Counter Intelligence Corps Detachment

Attachments

710th Tank Battalion (– Companies A and B)

483rd Antiaircraft Artillery Automatic Weapons Battalion (40mm/.50cal.)

HQ & HQ Company, 1138th Engineer Combat Group (– detachments)

481st Transportation Corps Amphibious Truck Company (– three detachments) (DUKW)

592nd Joint Assault Signal Company (– three detachments)

41st Medical Portable Surgical Hospital

one Photo Assignment Unit, 3116th Signal Service Battalion

Detachment, Translator-Interpreter Team A, HQ Company, Central Pacific Area (– three detachments)

1st Platoon, Provisional Quartermaster Graves Registration Company (– three detachments), 81st Inf. Div.

one platoon, 17th Medical Field Hospital

Garrison Force, Angaur

HQ, Garrison Force, Angaur

7th Antiaircraft Artillery Battalion (90/40/20mm) (USMC)

290th Transportation Corps Port Company

405th Ordnance Medium Maintenance Company

2d Platoon, 3259th Quartermaster Service Company

3d Platoon, 247th Quartermaster Depot Company

3d Depot Platoon, 722nd Engineer Depot Company

104th Bomb Disposal Squad

322nd, were to assault Angaur Island, but only when released by the 1st Mar. Div. commander once he considered the situation on Peleliu did not require the assistance of the 81st Infantry Division.

The 81st Inf. Div. had been reactivated at Camp Rucker, Alabama, in June 1942. It had served in France in World War I. The new division was raised from a small Regular Army 3rd Inf. Div. cadre filled with newly commissioned reserve officers and conscripted troops. After receiving desert training, participating in corps-level exercises stressing the attack of fortified positions, and then amphibious training in California, it transferred to Hawaii for additional amphibious training. It then went to Guadalcanal, now a large base, where it undertook jungle training. While the troops were acclimatized and undertook training in rugged terrain with limited visibility, it did little to specifically prepare them for Angaur and Peleliu. Angaur was to be its first combat action.

Army infantry regiments had 3,257 troops in a 108-man headquarters and headquarters company (with a platoon of three 37mm AT M3A1 guns

Marines of 3/1 dig in and take cover on White Beach while others move inland only to become pinned down by murderous Japanese fire from "The Point," the high ground seen here in the background. This obstacle appeared on none of the maps and held up 3/1's advance all day, defying all attempts to take it by frontal assault. The Point was only finally taken by K/3/1 after they worked their way around the flank and assaulted the Japanese positions from the rear.

and an intelligence and reconnaissance platoon), a 118-man cannon company with six 75mm M1A1 pack howitzers, a 165-man antitank company with nine 37mm AT guns plus a mine platoon, and a 115-man service company. Its three 871-man infantry battalions had a 155-man headquarters and headquarters company, three 193-man rifle companies, and a 160-man heavy-weapons company (D, H, M) with eight .30cal. M1917A1 heavy machine guns in two platoons and a platoon of six 81mm M1 mortars. The rifle companies had three 39-man rifle platoons with three 12-man rifle squads comprised of a squad leader (M1 rifle), assistant squad leader (M1 rifle), automatic rifleman (M1918A2 BAR), assistant automatic rifleman (M1 rifle), grenadier (M1 rifle, M7 grenade launcher), and seven riflemen (M1 rifles). The company had five 2.36in. M1A1 bazookas to be issued as it saw fit. The weapons platoon had a section with two .30cal. M1919A4 light machine guns and a section of three 60mm M2 mortars.

Army divisional artillery was organized differently from the Marine Corps'. The division artillery, commanded by a brigadier general, had three 105mm M2A1 howitzer battalions (316th, 317th, 906th Field Artillery Battalions) and one 155mm M1A1 howitzer battalion (318th). Each field artillery battalion had a headquarters and headquarters battery, service battery, and three howitzer batteries with four tubes apiece.

The attached 710th Tank Battalion had M4A1 Sherman tanks with 17 tanks each in Companies A–C, three platoons of five and two in the headquarters. Six 75mm M8 self-propelled howitzers were in the headquarters company's assault gun platoon. Company D, normally equipped with light tanks, had 3in. gun-armed M10 tank destroyers, which were invaluable for blasting out caves. The Army's amphibian tractor battalions, like the Marines, were equipped with LVT(2) and LVT(4) amtracs.

Assault troops for Operation Stalemate II numbered approximately 2,647 officers and 44,914 enlisted men, of whom 1,438 officers and 24,979 enlisted were Marines.

See page 34 for the 81st Inf. Div. organization for the Angaur (321st and 322nd RCTs) and Ulithi (323rd RCT) assaults.

JAPANESE FORCES – PALAU DISTRICT GROUP

The 4th Fleet was responsible for the defense of the Japanese Mandated Territory. There were submarine and seaplane bases on Arakabesan, another seaplane base on Koror, the islands' headquarters and administrative center, and airfields on Babelthuap, Peleliu, and Ngesebus. The 4th Fleet headquarters relocated to Truk in February 1942.

The 14th Division under LtGen Inoue Sadao arrived in the Palaus from Manchuria via Saipan in April 1944. The Division had been raised in 1905 and served in the Russo-Japanese War, the Siberian Expedition, and the Manchurian Incident. Between 1932 and 1944 it served three tours in China and Manchuria. In March 1944, just prior to its transfer to the Mandates, it was reorganized as an amphibious division. This organization, called a "regimental combat team division" by the Allies, was not intended for amphibious assault, but was optimized to operate on Pacific islands with the regiments structured to operate independently if need be. Artillery and engineer units were made organic to the regiment groups and an almost regimental-size sea transport unit was provided, equipped with 120 organic landing craft and barges. The regiment groups were of two different organizations. The 2nd Infantry was a Type A unit intended as a heavy strike force. The 15th and 57th Infantry were Type B light units. Details are vague on the internal organization of the regiments. They had three battalions each with three rifle companies, a machine gun company (six 7.7mm heavy machine guns), and an infantry gun company (two 37mm AT, two 70mm infantry guns), although it appears the Type A

"The Bloody Trail" – aptly named LVT(A)1 provides Marines on the landing beaches with fire support from its 37mm main armament and .30 and .50cal machine guns as well as much needed cover. Both gasoline and water were supplied to the troops in 5-gallon cans like the one shown in the center foreground. The sides of the cans were painted with a cross – yellow for gasoline and white for water. Water was also delivered in 55-gallon fuel drums, which had been improperly cleaned resulting in tainted water incapacitating many marines.

regiment's battalions had 81mm mortar companies instead. Both regiments had a battalion-sized artillery unit with nine 75mm guns in the Type A and 12 in the Type B. Distribution of other weapons is unclear, although this is actually a moot point as weapons were allocated to defense areas as necessary without regard to parent units. Both regiments had 112 7.7mm light machine guns and six 37mm AT guns with 114 50mm grenade dischargers ("knee mortars") in the Type A and 84 in the Type B. Additionally the Type A regiment had nine 20mm AT rifles, six 20mm machine cannons, numerous 81mm mortars, six flamethrowers, and nine light tanks in the tank unit. The strength figures below are the Allied estimated authorized strength and not necessarily the assigned strength.

14th Division Headquarters	300
2nd Infantry Regiment	3,960
15th Infantry Regiment	3,160
57th Infantry Regiment	3,160
14th Division Tank Unit	130
14th Division Signal Unit	235
14th Division Transport Unit	130
14th Division Sea Transport Unit	1,540
14th Division Intendant Service Unit	130
14th Division Ordnance Duty Unit	100
14th Division Water Supply & Purification Unit	160
14th Division Field Hospital	595

LtGen Inoue Sadao established his 14th Division headquarters on Koror Island, north of Peleliu, and doubled as Commander, Palaus District Group, assuming command of the 53rd Independent Mixed Brigade (IMB) and other IJA elements in the Palaus. After early aerial reconnaissance LtGen Inoue Sadao concluded that the islands of Peleliu, Ngesebus, and Angaur in the south of the Palaus chain would be the first of the islands to be assaulted by the Allies and as such would form the mainstay of his defense. It was for this reason that the heavy Type A 2nd Infantry was assigned to Peleliu. Most of the 59th Infantry was initially assigned to Angaur and the 15th Infantry to Babelthuap.

The 14th Division's 15th (-3rd Battalion) and 59th Infantry Regiments (-1st Battalion) defended Babelthuap along with the 53rd IMB (-346th Battalion), almost 21,000 troops and 10,000 Korean and Okinawan laborers. The 3,800-man 53rd IMB was commanded by MajGen Yamaguchi

Takso and had been organized from the 57th Line of Communications Sector Unit and the Sea Transport Unit of the 1st Amphibious Brigade on 30 May 1944. That brigade had been lost in the ill-fated defense of the Marshalls earlier in the year. Its five 580-man independent infantry battalions (the 347th was never raised) had a 37-man headquarters, three 114-man rifle companies, a 119-man machine gun company (12 7.7mm heavy machine guns), and an 82-man infantry gun company (two 37mm AT, two 70mm infantry guns). The rifle companies had three platoons of three 10-man sections (squads) each. Each section had a 7.7mm light machine gun and a 50mm grenade discharger. The battalion-sized artillery unit had three companies each with four 75mm field guns. It was mostly concentrated on Koror.

53rd Independent Mixed Brigade Headquarters	280
356th, 348th, 349th, 350th, and 351st Independent Infantry Battalions	580 each
53rd IMB Artillery Unit	415
53rd IMB Engineer Unit	220

Yap Island was defended by 4,000 troops of the 49th IMB, 3,000 IJN personnel of the 46th Base Force, and 1,000 laborers. Ulithi Atoll had supported an airfield and seaplane base, but had been abandoned by the Japanese several months before the US landing.

Col Nakagawa's 6,500-man IJA force on Peleliu was as follows:

2nd Infantry (Reinforced)	**Col Nakagawa**	
2nd Battalion, 2nd Infantry	Maj Tomita	242
3rd Battalion, 2nd Infantry	Capt Harada	635
3rd Battalion, 15th Infantry	Capt Chiaki	750
346th Independent Inf Bn, 53rd IMB	Maj Hikino	556
Sector Unit Reserve	*Capt Sakamoto*	
1st Battalion, 2nd Infantry	Capt Ichioka	635
1st Battalion, 818th Field Artillery[3]	Maj Kobayashi	unknown
14th Division Tank Unit[4]	Capt Amano	122
Engineer Company	Capt Isohata	250
Signal Unit	Capt Okada	180
Supply Company	1stLt Abe	160
Medical Company	1stLt Ando	160
Detachment, 14th Div. Field Hospital	1stLt Oya	117
Miscellaneous service attachments		120

---

3 The artillery battalion had eight 75mm guns and four 105mm howitzers.
4 The tank unit had 12–15 Model 95 medium tanks. The 14th Division Tank Unit and the 2nd Infantry Tank Unit may have been consolidated on Peleliu, but with small tank elements detached to Koror and Babelthuap.

Other IJA combat units on Peleliu included a light anti-aircraft unit; the 33rd, 35th, and 38th Machine Cannon Units with 20mm automatic guns; two 81mm mortar companies with 10 mortars each, and a 150mm mortar company with four mortars. This would be the Americans' first exposure to this devastating mortar. Most of the service and signal troops were reorganized into combat units themselves and used to augment infantry battalions once the invasion occurred.

IJN forces in the Palaus were under the command of the 30th Base Force after the departure of the 4th Fleet to Truk. Commanded by Vice-Admiral Ito Yoshioka, it consisted of the 43rd and 45th Guard Forces as well as air service, construction, and service troops. The IJN had by 1944

Marines of 2/1 move inland from Beach White 2 through heavy scrub heading for their first phase-line some 350 yards inland and bordering the airfield. This they reached by 0930hrs where they halted, waiting for 3/1 to move up alongside on their left – 3/1 being held up by "The Point."

constructed numerous reinforced concrete blockhouses and bunkers plus dug an extensive tunnel system near the end of the northeast peninsula as well as taking full advantage of Peleliu's natural caves. This elaborate, multi-level tunnel system could shelter 1,000 troops. These defenses, tunnels, the airfield, and the many support facilities were built by the 204th, 214th, and 235th(-) Construction Battalions, mostly manned by Koreans and Okinawans. Detachments of the guard forces manned eight 120mm dual-purpose, and about three 200mm coast defense guns. There was no ammunition for the 200mm short guns nor did any ships report being fired on by coast defense guns. The 114th and 126th Antiaircraft Units manned single and twin-barreled 25mm automatic guns (estimated at 30) and 13.2mm machine guns. A dozen 20mm cannons, removed from destroyed aircraft, were set up on makeshift mounts, mostly around the airfield. Also included were some 1,400 air base service personnel of the West Caroline Air Force. In all there were approximately 4,000 IJN personnel on Peleliu.

Angaur, the objective of the 81st Inf. Div. as part of Operation Stalemate II, was defended by the 1st Battalion, 59th Infantry (Reinforced), detached from the 14th Division and dubbed the Angaur Sector Unit, under the command of Major Ushio Goto. It mustered approximately 1,400 officers and enlisted men while American intelligence estimated Japanese forces on Angaur to be between 1,400 and 2,500 combat troops. The battalion was reinforced with a few IJN-manned 80mm coast defense guns, a 75mm mountain gun battery, a 20mm machine cannon company, 37mm and 47mm AT gun platoons, 81mm and 150mm mortar platoons, an engineer platoon, and service troops. Until late July the 59th Infantry, less one battalion, had garrisoned Angaur, but all but the 1st Battalion were withdrawn to defend Babelthuap.

Estimates vary, but there were approximately 21,000 IJA, 7,000 IJN, and 10,000 laborers in the Palau Islands.

PELELIU ASSAULT

D-DAY

15 September 1944 – D-Day on Peleliu. After an uneventful 2,100-mile voyage from their practice landings on Guadalcanal, men of the 1st Mar. Div. and the 81st Inf. Div. prepared for battle. In the pre-dawn light, on board troop transports, men checked and re-checked weapons and equipment. Breakfast of steak and eggs was a tradition that was often regretted by many a marine as he churned towards the beach in an amtrac or flat-bottomed Higgins boat – and cursed by many a ship's surgeon as he operated on the wounded. They climbed into LCVPs (Landing Craft, Vehicle and Personnel or "Higgins boat," after its inventor Andrew Higgins) and LVTs (Landing Vehicle, Tracked – better known as amphibian tractors or "amtracs").

Practice landings had demonstrated shortcomings, including troops hurriedly loaded onto wrong transports who had to be swapped over at sea. Above all, the area chosen for the practice landings did not have a fringing reef, so the often hazardous task of transferring from landing craft to amtrac could only be simulated and in no way demonstrated the rough sea conditions at a reef's edge. The practice landings resulted in several casualties from broken bones, including the Commanding General, 1st Mar. Div., MajGen Rupertus, with a broken ankle.

Starting three days earlier (12 September), frogmen of Underwater Demolition Teams (UDT) 6 and 7 began clearing submerged obstructions and blasting pathways through the reef for the assault troops. UDT 8 was

A wrecked DUKW lies totally destroyed on the beach after hitting one of the multitude of mines sown by Nakagawa's men on practically all potential landing sites. The resistance was far fiercer and vehicle losses higher than the Marines had expected.

7th Marines CP established in a large Japanese tank trap just inland from Beach Orange . This later became General Rupertus's first CP upon his landing on D+1.

doing the same at Angaur. This dangerous work was often carried out under direct small arms fire from the Japanese defending troops on the beaches. The Kossol Passage north of Babelthuap was swept for mines resulting in the loss of a minesweeper; a destroyer and another minesweeper were damaged in the effort.

At 0530hrs naval support ships had begun the pre-landing bombardment of the beaches from a range of 1,000 yards. This lifted at 0750hrs to make way for carrier-borne aircraft to strafe the beaches in front of the first landing waves, whilst the naval bombardment moved to targets inland. White phosphorous smoke shells were fired to screen the assault waves from the Japanese on the high ground inland to the north of the airfield.

The plan called for the first assault waves to be in amtracs. Subsequent support waves would transfer at the reef's edge from LCVPs to amtracs, returning from the beaches. This was basically the same plan as at Tarawa in 1943, and more than one marine had thoughts of their comrades in the 2nd Mar. Div. wading several hundred yards under murderous fire to the beaches when insufficient numbers of amtracs survived the return trip. This time, however, the first waves would be preceded by armored LVTs, which were specially produced amtracs with additional armor and a turreted 37mm gun, LVT(A)1, or 75mm howitzer LVT(A)4 to act as amphibious tanks to suppress beach defenses for the initial assault waves.

Preceding the first assault waves were 18 landing craft, infantry (gun) (LCI(G)) equipped with 4.5in. rocket launchers. Each of these fired a salvo of 72 rockets onto the beaches. When the third assault wave passed them, they retired to the flanks to deliver "on call" fire. In addition, four landing craft, infantry (mortar) (LCI[M])s armed with three

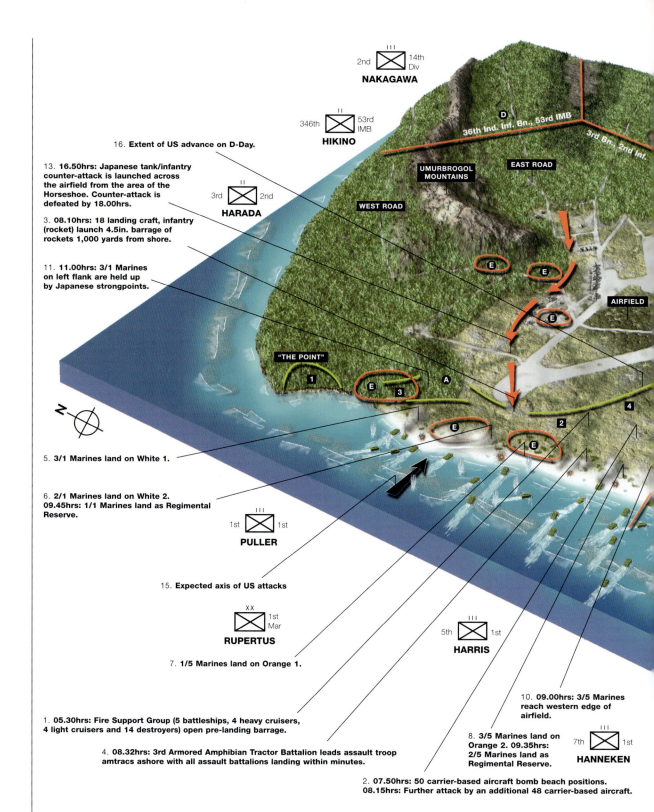

2nd 14th Div **NAKAGAWA**

346th 53rd IMB **HIKINO**

3rd 2nd **HARADA**

D

36th Ind. Inf. Bn., 53rd IMB

3rd Bn., 2nd Inf.

EAST ROAD

UMURBROGOL MOUNTAINS

WEST ROAD

16. **Extent of US advance on D-Day.**

13. **16.50hrs: Japanese tank/infantry counter-attack is launched across the airfield from the area of the Horseshoe. Counter-attack is defeated by 18.00hrs.**

3. **08.10hrs: 18 landing craft, infantry (rocket) launch 4.5in. barrage of rockets 1,000 yards from shore.**

11. **11.00hrs: 3/1 Marines on left flank are held up by Japanese strongpoints.**

AIRFIELD

"THE POINT"

1

E

3

A

E

E

E

4

2

N

5. **3/1 Marines land on White 1.**

6. **2/1 Marines land on White 2. 09.45hrs: 1/1 Marines land as Regimental Reserve.**

1st 1st **PULLER**

15. **Expected axis of US attacks**

x x 1st Mar **RUPERTUS**

7. **1/5 Marines land on Orange 1.**

5th 1st **HARRIS**

10. **09.00hrs: 3/5 Marines reach western edge of airfield.**

8. **3/5 Marines land on Orange 2. 09.35hrs: 2/5 Marines land as Regimental Reserve.**

7th 1st **HANNEKEN**

1. **05.30hrs: Fire Support Group (5 battleships, 4 heavy cruisers, 4 light cruisers and 14 destroyers) open pre-landing barrage.**

4. **08.32hrs: 3rd Armored Amphibian Tractor Battalion leads assault troop amtracs ashore with all assault battalions landing within minutes.**

2. **07.50hrs: 50 carrier-based aircraft bomb beach positions. 08.15hrs: Further attack by an additional 48 carrier-based aircraft.**

PELELIU – D-DAY

15 September 1944, viewed from the west showing the landings by 1st, 5th and 7th Marines, the push across the island and the Japanese counter-attacks.

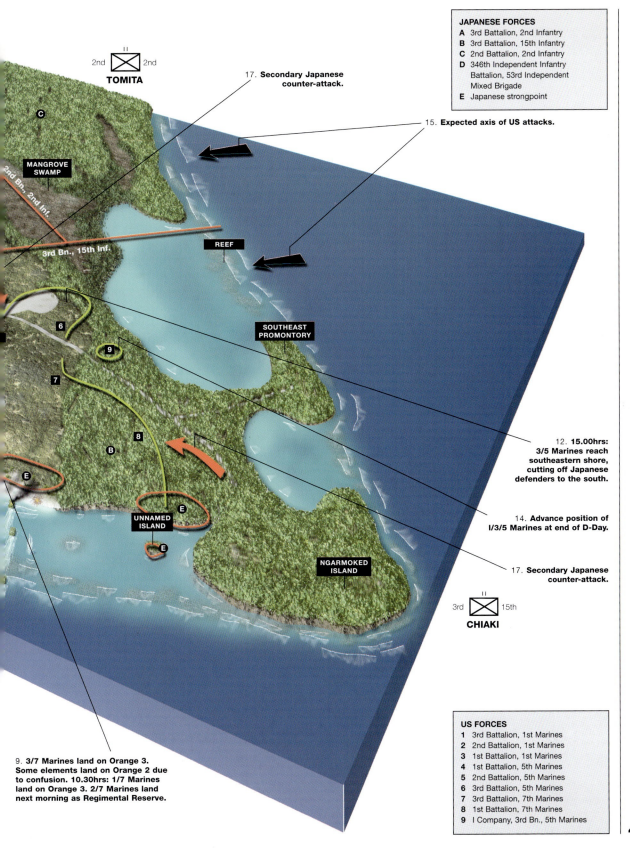

2nd ⊠ 2nd
TOMITA

17. **Secondary Japanese
counter-attack.**

15. **Expected axis of US attacks.**

**MANGROVE
SWAMP**

2nd Bn., 2nd Inf.

3rd Bn., 15th Inf.

REEF

6

9

7

**SOUTHEAST
PROMONTORY**

8

B

**UNNAMED
ISLAND**

E

E

E

E

**NGARMOKED
ISLAND**

12. **15.00hrs:
3/5 Marines reach
southeastern shore,
cutting off Japanese
defenders to the south.**

14. **Advance position of
I/3/5 Marines at end of D-Day.**

17. **Secondary Japanese
counter-attack.**

3rd ⊠ 15th
CHIAKI

9. **3/7 Marines land on Orange 3.
Some elements land on Orange 2 due
to confusion. 10.30hrs: 1/7 Marines
land on Orange 3. 2/7 Marines land
next morning as Regimental Reserve.**

4.2in. mortars, stood off the northern portion of Beach White to fire continuous salvos onto the area inland of the beach.

Admiral Oldendorf's confidence in his pre-assault bombardment proved misplaced. As the LVTs crossed the line of departure and raced for the beaches, it soon became apparent that there were still plenty of live Japanese on Peleliu. Artillery and mortar fire began to fall amongst the amtracs, several receiving direct hits; 26 were destroyed on D-Day. Smoke from the Japanese fire and burning amtracs, combined with the drifting smokescreen, completely obscured the beachhead for some time from the following assault waves and the transports off-shore.

An individual marine's account of what followed paints an almost surreal picture of how young men respond to the unprecedented fierceness of assaulting a well-defended beach.

Sterling Mace was a BAR-man in Company K, 3rd Battalion, 5th Marines (K/3/5). He was in one of the first waves to go in on Beach Orange 2. Twenty years after D-Day, he wrote:

"Into the ship's hold we descended to find the amphibian tractors waiting with their diesel engines roaring. The sound was deafening. The smell of the acrid fumes was sickening. The noise of the engines, men and equipment reverberated off the steel hull. We huddled, thirty-six men and a 37mm field piece to a tractor, waiting for the bow doors to open. Suddenly, the doors opened wide letting the dawn's light shed on us. Out the bay doors poured the 'Alligators,' which was a nickname for the amphibian tractors. One after another they splashed into the sea and, in full throttle, left the LST behind in its wake. I couldn't give you a count on the amount as I was not in a position to look over the bulkhead of the tractor I was in. We were jammed elbow to elbow. Not to mention the rise and fall in the waves. It seemed as if the 'Alligators' were like rubber balls bobbing up and down in the ocean swells. As we rode up one crest I caught a glimpse of several sailors on board the LST drinking from coffee mugs and watching us depart. I thought, then,

Seabees with heavy construction equipment intended for reconstructing the airfield on Peleliu first spend time clearing the beaches of debris and disabled LVTs and DUKWs. In addition to all their sophisticated weaponry the Marines also made use of some very simple technology such as the two-man handcart shown here, used by the US Marines since before WWI.

Aftermath of the Japanese armored counterattack on the afternoon of D-Day. The light Japanese Type 95 *Ha-Go* tanks were no match for the Marine artillery, anti-tank guns and particularly the Shermans. The Marines also had half-track-mounted 105mm guns, which were particularly useful against fixed defenses such as bunkers and pillboxes as well as tanks.

maybe I was in the wrong service. But looking at the faces of my buddies around me, I had mixed emotions. We had come so far together. I knew them. And to see their expressions of concern for themselves and each other, I was proud to be alongside of these men. Some were dead serious with furrows across their brows. Some were laughing and nervously joking. However, if the tractor made an uncommonly groan or hit a high peak of an underwater coral reef, the look of borderline panic would flush their faces.

"The amphibians began to circle and gradually drawing closer to the island. The beach master was organizing the numerical order of the tractors for the different waves to land and follow the battle plan. The 1st Marines was to land on our left. While the 7th [Marines] would be on our right. The 5th [Marines] would head straight, hitting Orange Beach 2. The beach was a little stretch of white sand with a backdrop of solid black smoke hiding the silhouette of tropical terrain of trees and mountains.

"Off in the distance a flag is waved and the amphibians turn their course toward the shore. Some 500 yards off shore were a line of LCIs launching 12,000 rockets onto the beach. The great battleships on the horizon are, also, firing away at the island. Someone in the outfit notices the tractor is fifteen yards in front of the main wave. Which brings about a chorus of 'Slow down! You're going too fast.' Nervous laughter.

"There comes the sound of grating sand and coral from the bottom of the tractor. The rear door drops down and we exit. One after another we step out, turn to the right or left to run toward the beach…"

Mace's feelings were typical of many Marines on D-Day.

The first Marines to hit the beaches were men of the 3rd Battalion, 1st Marines (3/1). They landed on Beach White 1 at 0832hrs, just 2 minutes behind schedule, and within the next 4 minutes there were Marines on all five landing beaches.

On Beach White the 1st Marines landed as planned, with the 2nd Battalion on the right and the 3rd on the left, with the 1st Battalion scheduled to land at approximately 0945hrs as regimental reserve.

BEACH ORANGE 3, 08.34HRS, D-DAY (pages 46–47)
On the extreme right flank of the beachhead, the 7th Marines came ashore in a column of battalions with 3rd in the lead. This battalion bore the full brunt of machine gun, antiboat gun, and mortar fire enfilading the beach from Unnamed and Ngarmoked Islands on Peleliu's south tip. LVT(4) amphibian tractors (1) were essential in delivering troops ashore as they carried more personnel than the earlier LVT(2)s, although these were used as well because of the shortages of LVT(4)s. This allowed five battalions to be landed by the first waves. The LVT(4) was the first LVT provided with a ramp. The firing wires for scores of command-detonated aerial bombs planted on the ⅞-mile wide reef had been cut by the bombardment sparing many amtracs. Indirect fire had inflicted little damage on the amtracs, but as they neared the beach large-caliber automatic weapons (13.2mm, 20mm, 25mm) and antiboat guns began to take their toll. 26 LVTs were knocked out on the first day with dozens damaged. As the LVTs came ashore the troops shoved ammunition boxes (2) and water cans (3) over the sides. These were to be picked up later by litter-bearers returning to the frontline after evacuating casualties. Two deficiencies encountered by the Marines on Peleliu were insufficient replacement combat troops and inadequate medical support. One reason for this is that it was expected that the island would be secured within five days. What was available was stretched to support the Marines' 44-day fight. Only two approximately 150-man replacement companies were deployed. They were attached to the 1st Pioneer Battalion as Companies D and E to assist with unloading until D+3 (9 September) when they were released as replacements to the regiments. They proved inadequate to replace the losses suffered by that date. Company C, 1st Tank Battalion deployed without its tanks and served as replacement crews. No more replacements were forthcoming for the remainder of battle. This forced the relief of the 1st Marines on D+16 (22 September) by the Army's 321st Infantry and the relief of the 1st Mar. Div. by the 81st Inf. Div. between 15 and 20 October. Two approximately 1,350-man replacement drafts were later attached to each Marine division landing on Iwo Jima and Okinawa, but even these proved inadequate. The Division relied on organic medical support. Each infantry battalion possessed a two-officer, 42-enlisted man aid station manned by Navy personnel. Medical corpsmen (4) from this element were attached to rifle platoons and also operated small rifle company aid stations. The infantry regiments each had an aid station with five officers and 19 enlisted men. While mostly Navy personnel, it had five Marine drivers for the ¼-ton jeep ambulances. A 102-man medical company was attached to each combat team for additional support, which in-turn attached a clearing section to each battalion to support the aid station. Company B, 1st Motor Transport Battalion deployed without its vehicles to serve as litter bearers and a 29-man band section was attached to each combat team for the same purpose. There were no higher echelon medical units ashore. Casualties were evacuated to troop transports by landing craft and amtrac. Well-equipped surgical hospitals were operated aboard these ships. (Howard Gerrard)

On White 2, the 2/1 landed successfully and proceeded to push inland against Japanese resistance described in their after-action report as "moderate." The 2/1 advanced, supported by some of the armored LVTs until their M4A2 Sherman tanks could get ashore, to reach a line approximately 350 yards inland through heavy woods by 0930hrs. Their hour's progress was not without casualties. Here 2/1 halted, at the far side of the woods and facing the airfield and buildings area. Tying in with the 5th Marines on their right flank, they held pending a solution to the problems the 3/1 were facing.

As soon as 3/1 hit Beach White 1, they faced stubborn and violent opposition from strongly emplaced Japanese small arms fire to their immediate front, as well as from artillery and mortar fire that was blanketing the whole beach area. To make matters worse, no sooner had the lead elements of 3/1 landed and advanced less than 100 yards inland, than they found themselves confronted by a most formidable natural obstacle, a rugged coral ridge, some 30ft high. This had not shown up on any maps. Worse, the face of this ridge (christened "The Point" by the Marines) was honeycombed with caves and firing positions which the Japanese had blasted into the coral and had turned into excellent defensive positions which resisted all initial assaults. Even after tanks arrived to support the assault troops attempting to storm the northern portion of the ridge, they stumbled into a wide, deep anti-tank ditch, dominated by the ridge itself. Here they came under severe and accurate enfilading fire and were pinned down for hours.

A/1/1 of the regimental reserve battalion was committed early in the day to support 3/1, followed by B/1/1 late in the afternoon. Still, all efforts failed to close the gap which had developed on the left. Late in the afternoon, a foothold was gained on the southern area of the point, which improved the situation somewhat. But the situation still gave great cause for concern, compounded by the fact that five LVTs carrying the

1st Marines command group had been badly hit whilst crossing the reef, with resultant loss of communications equipment and operators. Only much later in the day did divisional command become fully aware of the precariousness of the 1st Marines' position.

After more than eight hours of possibly the most fierce fighting of the Pacific War so far, two gaps in the 1st Marines' lines were so serious as to endanger the entire Division's position on D-Day. Indeed, so precarious was the situation that all possible reserves were committed, including headquarters personnel and at least 100 men from the 1st Engineer Battalion. Together they formed a defense in depth against the threat of a Japanese counterattack that could possibly roll up the entire line and sweep down the now congested landing beaches. Fortunately for the Marines, no such counterattack was planned by the Japanese.

It became apparent to the Marines that The Point was unassailable from the front and so eventually units fought inland and assaulted The Point from the rear. These units, commanded by Capt George P. Hunt, fought their way along The Point for nearly two hours, during which time they succeeded in neutralizing all of the enemy infantry protecting the major defensive blockhouses and pill boxes. The principal defense installation was a reinforced concrete casement built into the coral, mounting a 25mm automatic cannon, which had been raking the assault beaches all morning. This blockhouse was taken from above by Lieutenant William L. Willis, who dropped a smoke grenade outside the blockhouse's embrasure, to cover the approach of his men, and Corporal Anderson who launched a rifle grenade through the firing aperture. This disabled the gun and ignited the ammunition inside the blockhouse. After a huge explosion, the fleeing Japanese defenders were mown down by waiting Marine riflemen.

Capt Hunt and his surviving 30 or so men would remain isolated on The Point for the next 30 hours, all the time under attack from Japanese infiltrators trying to take advantage of the gap in Company K's lines. When relieved, Hunt only had 18 men standing to defend The Point and Company K had in total only 78 men remaining out of 235.

In the center, on beaches Orange 1 and 2, the 5th Marines fared a little better. The deadly antiboat fire on the way in had been less effective than elsewhere, though they too suffered losses in assault boats and amtracs from artillery and mortar fire.

1/5 landed on Orange 1 and 3/5 on Orange 2. On both beaches they met only scattered resistance, and little more as they moved inland. Instead of the unmapped coral ridges faced by the 1st Marines, the 5th Marines advanced through coconut groves which afforded ample cover, reaching their first objective line and tying in with 2/1 on the left by 0930hrs in front of the airfield.

A bizarre detail of Orange 2 was recalled by Sterling Mace:

"There, as we're heading towards shore, a small dog is wagging its tail and barking at us. The sound of the dog's bark is suddenly unheard as the tractor's gunner opens fire. His fifty caliber machine gun blazing away at the vegetation along the beachfront. The last time we saw the dog, the little guy was in a mad dash down the beach…

"In the time it took from the amphibian tractor in the surf to the beach everything was in mass confusion."

Here, 1/5 halted. Partly, this was because of the lack of progress by the 1st Marines on the extreme left against The Point, and partly due to the murderous Japanese artillery and mortar fire which was sweeping the airfield and open ground to their immediate front.

On Orange 2, 3/5 did not fare as well as 1/5 on Orange 1. Lieutenant Colonel Austin C. Shoftner, commander of 3/5, lost his executive officer Major Robert Ash within minutes of landing, killed by Japanese artillery fire. The LVT carrying most of the battalion's communications equipment and personnel was also destroyed on the reef.

According to plan, Company I landed on the left and Company K on the right, with Company L landing shortly afterwards as battalion reserve. On the left, all went comparatively well with Company I making contact with 1/5 and advancing inland along with them.

On the right however, Company K ran into difficulties when elements of the 7th Marines landed on beach Orange 2 instead of landing on their intended beach of Orange 3. This caused some confusion on the beach and delayed Company K's advance. They did not draw abreast of Company I until 1000hrs.

The 3rd Battalion's situation deteriorated somewhat after the advance inland was resumed at 1030hrs. Company K advanced through fairly dense scrub which provided concealment from the Japanese shelling. As a result they began to pull ahead of Company I and eventually broke contact with them. Company L was committed in an effort to close the gap, but this line remained dangerously extended for most of D-Day. By the afternoon, the regimental reserve, 2/5, had landed and it relieved Company I who in turn were ordered to pass around Company L and tie in with them and Company K. Easier ordered than done as there was some confusion due to the poor quality of the maps of that area.

More bad luck befell the 3rd Battalion when, at about 1700hrs, a Japanese mortar barrage struck the command post. Colonel Shofner and several other members of the command staff were wounded and had to be evacuated, which severely disrupted the effectiveness of the 3rd Battalion as a unit.

Lieutenant Colonel Lewis W. Walt, executive officer of the 5th Marines, assumed command of the 3rd Battalion, but it was after dark before he located even the first of his companies. It would take him all night to restore any semblance of order in the 3rd Battalion.

By the end of D-Day, the front of the 5th Marines presented a rather odd appearance with the three Battalions facing east, north and south and the 2nd and 3rd Battalions virtually back to back, but strange as this seemed they were well enough integrated to present more than adequate defense for the night.

On the extreme right the 7th Marines were to land on Beach Orange 3 with two battalions in column. The third battalion, 2/7, was kept afloat as the divisional reserve.

The 3rd Battalion landed first. The 1st Battalion was to land shortly afterwards, but they encountered serious difficulties. The reef off Orange 3 was so cluttered with natural and man-made obstacles that the amtracs ended up approaching the beach in column, thus slowing the attack and also making them prime targets for Japanese antiboat fire, which was poured into them from Ngarmoked Island on the southwest of the landing beaches, in addition to the heavy artillery and mortar fire from inland on Peleliu.

This situation caused many amtrac drivers to veer off to the left, resulting in them landing on Orange 2 instead of Orange 3, creating the confusion experienced by 3/5. Extricating 3/7 was further complicated by land mines and barbed wire entanglements, so much valuable time was lost in getting the 7th Marines back on course. The 3/11 lost an entire 105mm battery on D-Day and was forced to re-embark and land again the next day as its firing positions were still in enemy hands.

Once again, as with the 1st Marines, there was a substantial obstacle in front of the 7th Marines that was not on any maps. This time, however, it would prove most useful. This obstacle took the form of a large anti-tank ditch just a short distance inland of Orange 3. It had only been spotted by the pilot of one of the planes observing the landings, who flashed a report back to Divisional HQ. The ditch proved most useful for moving troops forward in relative safety and provided a superb instant dugout for the battalion command post (CP).

The 3rd Battalion advanced inland, with Company K on the right and Company I on the left, and linked up with 3/5 advancing inland from Orange 2.

By 1045hrs Company K's advance had covered some 500 yards and they had also captured a Japanese radio direction finder in the process. Company I on the other hand had run into stiff Japanese resistance and were halted by a complex of blockhouses and gun emplacements in the ruins of the Japanese barracks area. Here Company I halted to await the arrival of tank support. This tank support became somewhat confused by an unexpected coincidence: the flank battalions of the two assaulting regiments in the center and right were both the 3rd (3/5 and 3/7) with both containing Companies I, K, and L. The unfortunate tank commanders looking for 3/7 who had wandered into 3/5 area due to obstacles – in particular the large antitank ditch on Orange 3 – enquired

M4A2 Sherman tanks advance across the airfield supporting the main advance to the south and east. In the background can be seen the Japanese aircraft hangars.

of a body of troops they encountered "is this Company I, 3rd Battalion?" Hearing the right answer in the wrong place, they proceeded to operate with these troops, who were in fact Company I of 3/5 and not Company I of 3/7. Happily, this was one of those confusions of battle that helped more than it hindered.

The confusion resulted in a gap between the two regiments as 3/7 paused to take stock of the situation, whereas 3/5 was actually pushing ahead. In an effort to re-establish contact with 3/5, Company L worked patrols further and further to the left until its foremost patrol emerged on the southern edge of the airfield. This was completely out of its regimental zone of action and several hundred yards to the rear of the units it was looking for.

In the meantime, 1/7 had landed as planned on Orange 3 at 1030hrs with slightly more success than 3/7, although some elements still ended up on Orange 2. Resistance was initially described as "light," but when the Battalion wheeled right as per plan, Japanese resistance increased notably. Once again poor maps let the Marines down. This time a dense swamp, not shown on any map, confronted the right half of the battalion and the only trail round it was heavily defended. It took considerable time to work around the swamp and it was not until 1520hrs that Col Gormley was able to confirm reaching his objective line. During the night the battalion would receive a strong Japanese counter-attack from the swamp, which was defeated only with the aid of Black Marine shore party personnel who volunteered as riflemen.

The lack of progress on the right worried General Rupertus aboard the USS *Du Page* (APA-41) and his concern over the loss of momentum resulted in him first committing the divisional reconnaissance company ashore and later still attempting to commit the divisional reserve.

Gains for the Marines on D-Day were disappointing compared to the optimistic predictions. The 1st and 5th Marines had fallen short of their targets and the 7th Marines were the only ones to make any reasonable progress inland. The gap that remained in the middle of 3/5 on the left posed a threat to the entire south facing line.

JAPANESE TANK COUNTER-ATTACK, 16.50HRS, D-DAY
(pages 54–55)

The expected Japanese counter-attack on the landing force was launched from north of the airfield, the area in the southeast portion of the Umubrogol Mountains that would become known as the Horseshoe. A rifle company of 1st Battalion, 2nd Infantry and the 14th Division Tank Company launched the Japanese attack towards 1st Battalion, 5th Marines. The Japanese tanks raced ahead of their supporting infantry, although some infantrymen (1) were unfortunate enough to ride on the back of tanks – some tanks had been fitted with bamboo handrails on the engine deck for the riflemen to cling to. The attack was doomed from the start as it was executed too late. This was an error the Japanese frequently made; rather than attacking into the first assault waves as they landed on the beaches under heavy fire and were still disorganized, the Japanese waited until the Americans had tanks ashore along with more troops and had consolidated. On Peleliu Marine tanks had already been landed and were in position waiting. An extremely confused battle erupted as the Japanese tanks charged across the airfield. Their sheer momentum carried a few through the Marine line and into the rear, but Marine casualties were very light. All but two Japanese tanks were destroyed as eight M4A2 Sherman tanks (2) of Companies A and B, 1st Tank Battalion joined the fray. At least half of the Japanese infantry was wiped out in this poorly coordinated attack. It has never been accurately determined how many Japanese tanks were

destroyed, but reports indicate between 11 and 17. By totaling the claims of Japanese tanks killed in unit after action reports, one Marine staff officer calculated that 179½ tanks had been knocked out. The Type 95 (1935) *Ha-Go* light tanks (3) were vulnerable to virtually all Marine weapons over .30cal having only 6–12mm (0.24 to 0.47in.) of armor. Armed with the 37mm Type 94 (1934) gun (4), the tank also mounted a 7.7mm Type 97 (1937) machine gun in the left bow of the hull (5) and another in the rear of the turret. It carried 130 high explosive and armor-piercing-high explosive rounds plus 2,970 rounds of 7.7mm in 30-round magazines. The Type 95 was one of the most numerous tanks produced by Japan. While much an improvement over the Type 93 (1933), this 10-ton tank's capabilities and design fell far short of contemporary US and European light tanks. One of its main problems was the one-man turret, which left the tank commander to observe for enemy activity in all directions, determine his route, maintain his place in the formation, watch the platoon or company commander's tank for signals, load and fire the main gun and the rear machine gun, and direct the driver and bow machine-gunner. The short-barreled 37mm gun was of comparatively low velocity and lacked the armor penetration of US 37mm guns. Even though they had the same designation, its ammunition was not interchangeable with that of the 37mm Type 94 (1934) infantry antitank gun having a smaller cartridge case. The Type 95 tank's one good point was that its 6-cylinder diesel engine provided it with sufficient power and speed. (Howard Gerrard)

During the night, coordinated local counter-attacks were beaten off with little difficulty, thanks in part to naval gunfire and star shells combining with the artillery of the 11th Marines. These were not the expected suicidal *banzai* attacks, but took a more coherent form; the first time the Americans had experienced this sort of attack.

One major Japanese counterattack occurred at around 1650hrs on D-Day, consisting of a tank-infantry sortie in force across the northern portion of the airfield. This attack had been expected by the Marines, especially those of the 5th Marines facing open ground in front of the airfield, and accordingly the regimental commanders had brought up artillery and heavy machine guns as well as tanks to support that area.

Increase in Japanese artillery and mortar fire in that area was the first indication that something was brewing. Soon after Japanese infantry was observed advancing across the airfield, not as a fanatical, drunken *banzai* charge but as a coolly disciplined advance of veteran infantrymen. A Navy air observer spotted Japanese tanks forming east of the ridges above the airfield with more infantry riding on them. These tanks moved forward, passing through the Japanese infantry advancing across the airfield and some 400 yards in front of the Marine lines. For a moment, but only for a moment, the Japanese counter-attack looked like a serious coordinated movement. Then the formation went to pieces. Inexplicably, the Japanese tank drivers opened their throttles wide and raced towards the Marine lines. Charging like the proverbial "Bats outa Hell," with the few infantry atop the tanks clinging on for dear life, they left their accompanying infantry foot support far behind.

No positive account exists of what happened thereafter. The tanks involved in the charge numbered between 13 and 17 (insufficient pieces were left afterwards to give a definite count) and headed for the Marine lines, cutting diagonally across the front of 2/1, who subjected them to murderous flanking fire from all weapons, small arms, light and heavy machine guns, 37mm antitank guns and artillery. Two of the Japanese tanks veered off into the lines of 2/1, hurtling over a coral embankment and crashing into a swamp, the escaping crews were quickly disposed of by the Marines.

Meantime, the remaining tanks came under heavy fire from the marines of 1/5, while the advancing Japanese infantry was subjected to fire and bombing from a passing Navy dive bomber.

The tanks and their riding infantry were decimated as they passed right through the Marine lines which simply closed behind them. Exactly who knocked out what is, to this day, a mystery. Only two of the Japanese tanks escaped the massacre, although if all confirmed hits were taken into account the Japanese tank force must have numbered some 180 tanks!

As for the Japanese infantry, when the Marines looked back after the tanks had broken through their lines, the Japanese infantry was nowhere in sight. Whether they had been annihilated by the devastating Marine fire or whether they withdrew after seeing their tank support being decimated remains conjecture but the counterattack was over. It is doubtful we shall ever learn the definitive answer.

Several more smaller counterattacks occurred up and down the line during the afternoon of D-Day, none of which amounted to much except for one at about 1730hrs when infantry, supported by two tanks

The aftermath of one of the many counterattacks by the Japanese during the fighting around the airfield. These were not the frenzied *banzai* attacks as experienced previously by the Marines, but coordinated small-scale attacks, probing the Marine lines, though the outcome was usually the same.

(probably the two that escaped earlier), attacked the lines of the 1st and 5th Marines. Both tanks were destroyed and the Japanese infantry failed to reach the Marine lines.

One thing was noted by the Marines with regard to the Japanese counter-attacks and that was the fact that these were coordinated and disciplined attacks, rather than the frenzied *banzai* suicide charges experienced before. This was the first indication that something different was in store for the attacking Marines on Peleliu.

D+1 TO D+7

General Rupertus and his staff landed on D+1 at 0950hrs and took over direction of operations, taking over the command post that General D.P. Smith had set up in the large antitank ditch just inland of Beach Orange 2 on D-Day. This was a somewhat uncomfortable position for General Rupertus, as the area was still under Japanese fire from time to time and particularly as his leg and broken ankle were still in a plaster cast.

Nevertheless, plans were drawn up, based on the original battle plan for the advance across the island, in spite of the fact that the D-Day objectives had not been achieved and Puller's 1st Marines on the left flank were in serious trouble.

On the right flank (south) the 7th Marines were to advance east and south. The 1st Battalion was anchored on the western shore at Beach Orange 3 and the 3rd Battalion was inland, but held up by a large Japanese reinforced concrete blockhouse, which they had not been able to reduce before nightfall on D-Day. At 0800hrs the 3/7 resumed their assault on the blockhouse, this time with the assistance of naval gunfire and tanks, but the blockhouse was only finally reduced by direct assault from demolition teams under a smokescreen. Company I reached the eastern shore at approximately 0925hrs and proceeded to dig in against possible counterlandings from the Japanese on Koror or Babelthuap, which were a definite possibility.

In the meantime, the 1/7 attacked southwards over terrain described as "low and flat" (Intelligence described almost all of Peleliu as low and

flat). This was covered with scrub overgrowth that hampered progress. Most of the Japanese defenses in this area faced seaward in the anticipation of this area being part of possible landing beaches and, as such, 1/7 were assaulting these defenses from their less protected flanks and rear. Nevertheless, the area was still honeycombed with casemates, blockhouses, bunkers and pillboxes, all mutually supporting with trenches and rifle pits with well-cleared fields of fire for rifles and machine guns.

The going was grim and deadly but once again the Japanese had no intention of giving up lightly. They made the Marines pay dearly for every inch of Peleliu. 1/7 pushed forwards, supported by naval gunfire, air strikes and medium tanks; men from K/3/7 reached the southern shore around 1025hrs.

One other factor hampering the Marines' progress was the temperature on Peleliu. During the day, it was over 100°F and the strains of protracted fighting and dehydration were beginning to tell.

A wounded Marine gets a most welcome drink from a buddy. Temperatures were over 100°F during the day and drinking water was always in short supply. Initial supplies of water landed came in drums previously used for storing gasoline and inadequately cleaned. Many marines suffered the effects of drinking the tainted water.

The advance was halted around 1200hrs until water and fresh supplies could be brought up. Unfortunately for the Marines, the drums the water was brought to them in had previously been used to store aviation fuel and had not been properly cleaned. This was to temporarily incapacitate many of the much-needed Marine infantrymen.

The rest of D+1 was spent bringing up supplies, together with tanks which assisted in reducing the remaining Japanese defenses, while covering engineers clearing the profusion of mines which had been planted on the beach, this being the only approach by land.

D+2 saw the 7th Marines pushing further south, assaulting the southeast and southwest promontories of the southern shore. 3/7 were to assault the southeast promontory but the jump-off was delayed from 0800 to 1000hrs after another minefield was discovered and had to be cleared by the engineers. Then, after an artillery and mortar barrage, Company L advanced supported by three medium tanks. By 1026hrs a foothold was gained and, after some fierce fighting, the area was secured. The entire promontory was taken by 1320hrs.

The southwestern promontory, much larger than the southeastern promontory, was the target of 1/7. They launched their assault at 0835hrs, with the Marines meeting stiff resistance from the start. Progress was halted while tanks and armored LVT(A)s were brought up and artillery pounded the Japanese defenses. The attack resumed at 1430hrs. This time they succeeded in taking the Japanese first line of defense. Although resistance was stubborn and progress was slow, by nightfall of D+2 half of the promontory was in Marine hands.

During the night of D+2/D+3, additional armor (tanks and 75mm gun-mounted halftracks) was brought up and at 1000hrs of D+3 the advance was resumed. Again progress was painfully slow with many reserve elements being attacked by Japanese from bypassed caves and underground emplacements. At 1344hrs elements of Companies A and C reached the southern shores, though the area being assaulted by Company B was still heavily defended. Tank support had withdrawn to re-arm and before Company B was in a position to resume the attack, a bulldozer was needed to extricate the gun-mounted half-tracks, which had become bogged down. At that time, several explosions were heard from the Japanese defenses and it was found that remaining Japanese defenders had finished the job for the Marines. The final handful leaped from the cliff tops into the sea in an effort to escape, only to be picked off by Marine riflemen.

With the taking of the two promontories, the southern part of Peleliu was secured. 1/7 and 3/7 squared themselves away for a well-earned rest, while headquarters reported "1520 hours D+3, 7th Marines mission on Peleliu completed." Unfortunately, this was not quite the case.

Whilst the 7th Marines were successfully securing the south, the 5th Marines in the center prepared to expand on their gains of D-Day. On D+1 the 5th Marines were to push east across the airfield and then swing northeast, pivoting on the 1st Marines' left flank. In little over an hour 1/5 swept the entire northern area of the airfield with the only serious resistance coming from a series of emplacements around the hangar area. This area was secured by late afternoon of D+1, but only after heavy fighting and the front line having to be drawn back to a large anti-tank ditch for the night.

Meanwhile, 2/5, advancing on 1/5's right flank, was making slow progress against open ground and heavy Japanese resistance. Furthermore, on the east of the airfield, woods gave way to a mangrove swamp. Both the woods and swamp were infested with Japanese emplacements which had to be reduced by costly hand-to-hand fighting. But, by nightfall of D+1, 2/5 was alongside and tied in with 1/5, ready for the next day's advance.

Because of the advances of 2/5 on its left and the 7th Marines on its right, 3/5 was practically pinched out of operations on D+1, reduced to securing its positions along the shoreline and assisting 2/5 and 3/7 where possible. Colonel Walt, who had taken over temporary command

As the Marines pushed inland they encountered varying terrain from dense underbrush, as here, to swamps, grasslands and eventually mountains. The terrain on Peleliu made the island a defender's dream and the Japanese used it to full advantage.

A Marine "war dog" handler
reads a message he has just
received from his canine
dispatch runner. War dogs were
used extensively by the Marines
throughout the Pacific, they were
excellent at carrying messages
as here, and also made superb
lookouts, soon picking up the
scent of any approaching
Japanese infiltrators.

of 3/5, was replaced by Maj John H. Gustafson and returned to his post of Regimental Executive Officer, 5th Marines.

D+2 saw the 5th Marines advancing to the northeast, but they began to come under flanking fire from Japanese positions on the high ground to the front of the 1st Marines. 1/5 reached its objectives by mid-morning of D+2 where it held until relieved by 3/5. But when 3/5 tried to resume the advance in the afternoon it became pinned down from heavy flanking fire on its left.

On the right, 2/5 had more success being concealed in the woods from Japanese artillery and mortar fire.

Resistance on the ground was light and 2/5 was able to advance to beyond its objective line, though the heat and terrain began to take their toll on the Marines. Frequent halts had to be called, but by nightfall of D+2, 2/5 was tied in with 3/5 on the left and the shoreline on the right.

D+3 (18 September) saw the 5th Marines making slow but continuous progress. On the left, the regimental boundary was the road that skirted the high ground of the Umurbrogol Mountains, which were giving Puller's 1st Marines so much trouble. On the right, things were much different. Jumping off at 0700hrs, 2/5 hacked its way through dense jungle scrub, encountering only scattered resistance. Within two hours lead elements reached an improved road heading eastwards to the shores of Peleliu's northeastern peninsula. This road was so closely bordered by swamps as to become a causeway which could be perilous to an advance. A patrol was therefore sent in advance of the main body and, drawing no fire, an air strike was called in advance of a crossing in force.

Unfortunately the air strike missed completely so an artillery barrage was called for. Following this, elements of Companies G and F began crossing the causeway. Then, from out of the blue, came another unexpected air strike which strafed the advancing Marines, resulting in 34 casualties from "friendly fire."

Nevertheless the bridgehead was established, but suffered further casualties from misplaced friendly artillery and mortar fire. With this new tactical opening, Regimental HQ shifted 3/5 (leaving Company L tied in with the 1st Marines) eastwards across the causeway to assist 2/5. By nightfall of D+3 they had a bridgehead north and east, facing the main Ngardololok installations shown on Marine maps and in reports as the "RDF area" as it contained a radio direction finder station.

On D+4 2/5 and 3/5 advanced on the RDF area against only light resistance from scattered Japanese stragglers, most of whom chose to hide rather than fight. Both battalions pushed on and by the end of D+4 3/5 had reached the eastern shoreline and later the southern shores (designated Beach Purple). By D+6 they had secured the whole peninsula, while 2/5 continued east and north stopping short of Island A (an islet just off the causeway) which proved to be deserted. This discovery was made by a patrol sent across the previous day (D+5). 2/5 then pushed further north to the second, larger island of Ngabad, again without opposition.

But on the Division's left flank things were going far from well. Puller's 1st Marines had, from the outset on D-Day, run up against fierce, well-coordinated resistance from what would prove to be the main Japanese defenses in depth, centered around the Umurbrogol Mountains.

On D+1 MajGen Rupertus, upon arriving at the beachhead command post, ordered 2/7 (the division reserve) transferred to Puller's hard-pressed 1st Marines in an effort to "maintain momentum," as Rupertus would say to Puller many times.

2/1 was facing east and on D+1 swung left (north) to take the built-up area between the airfield and the mountains. This they achieved, crossing

On the 1st Marines' front the fighting was murderous from the beginning. Here Marines gently pass a wounded comrade down to receive treatment from the ever-present navy corpsmen. Note the rifle grenade in the foreground, a very useful weapon against bunkers and caves.

the airfield within half an hour. On the left, however, 3/1 was unable to advance at all and the regimental reserve, 1/1, was committed in the afternoon to assist. After bitter fighting, Marine infantry supported by tanks captured a 500-yard segment of the ridge and Company B was able to make contact with Company K which had been isolated for some 30 hours. A concerted counterattack by the Japanese on the night of D+1 was beaten off, but the hard fighting had taken a toll. By the morning of D+2, Company K was down to 78 men remaining from the original 235 and was ordered to the rear into reserve.

On D+2 elements of the 1st Marines came into contact for the first time with the Umurbrogol Mountains. Aerial photographs did little justice to the real nature of the mountains described later in the 1st Marines regimental narrative thus:

"a contorted mass of coral, strewn with rubble crags, ridges and gulches".

By D+2 the 1st Marines had already suffered over 1,000 casualties and as a result all three battalions were assembled in line on the regimental front, 3/1 on the left flank, 1/1 in the center and 2/1 on the right flank, with the newly arrived 2/7 in reserve.

2/1 were the first to encounter the Umurbrogol defenses, being stopped dead in their tracks after initial good progress by the first of many ridges (this one christened Hill 200). The men of 2/1 scaled the slopes and, after bitter hand-to-hand fighting and many casualties, by nightfall of D+2 had secured the crest of Hill 200 but immediately came under fire from the next ridge (Hill 210), thus the pattern was set.

In the center, 1/1 progressed well, until confronting a substantial reinforced concrete blockhouse, unmarked by naval gunfire, and which had previously been reported "destroyed" by Admiral Oldendorf in his pre-invasion bombardments. This complex was only taken after fire control parties called in fire from naval 14in. guns directly onto the emplacements.

On the left the picture was a little brighter as 3/1 was able to advance along the comparatively flat coastal plain but had to call a halt when it was in danger of losing contact with 1/1 on its right flank.

By D+3 Puller's 1st Marines had suffered 1,236 casualties yet Puller was still being urged on by MajGen Rupertus to "maintain the momentum" and, as a result, all available reserves including pioneers, engineers, and headquarters personnel were committed as infantrymen. Also 2/7, the division reserve, moved in to replace 1/1 in the center, which went into reserve. D+3 was a repeat of D+2 and would be repeated day after day. 2/1 took Hill 210, whilst the Japanese counter-attacked Hill 200, forcing the Marines to withdraw. In the afternoon, 2/1's situation was so desperate that Company B, 1/1, having just gone into reserve, was sent to assist 2/1 assaulting yet another ridge (Hill 205). This hill turned out to be isolated so Company B pushed on but was thrown back by a complex of defenses that was to become known as "Five Sisters." On the left once again 3/1 fared best, advancing along the coastal plains, halting again to maintain contact with 2/7 in the center.

After a harrowing night of counterattacks what was left of the 1st Marines plus 2/7 re-assumed the attack on D+4 after a naval and artillery barrage. Once again progress was best on the left, 3/1 pushing forward but again having to halt. In the center, 2/7 slogged from ridge

BELOW **"Lady Luck takes a nose-dive" – this LVT(A)4 found a novel way of dealing with this Japanese navy gun, although getting bogged down in soft sand in so doing. However, the Japanese gun and crew have clearly come off worse in the encounter.**

Men of the 7th Marines, loaded down with weaponry and personal equipment, move up to relieve Chesty Puller's 1st Marines. Puller's almost superhuman efforts to comply with Gen Rupertus's orders to "maintain momentum" resulted in the 1st Marines suffering staggering casualties on Peleliu, amounting to over 70 per cent killed or wounded.

to ridge suffering heavy casualties and 2/1 on the right pushed on over similar terrain against stiff resistance, which got worse with each successive ridge.

Although 2/1 did not know it, they were attacking what was to become the final Japanese pocket in the Umurbrogol Mountains.

By the end of D+4 the 1st Marines existed in name only, having suffered almost 1,749 casualties – six fewer casualties than the entire 1st Mar. Div. lost on Guadalcanal. On D+6, after another day of bitter hand-to-hand fighting, Puller was visited by IIIAC commanding general, Roy Geiger. Upon his return to Division Headquarters, after seeing first hand the condition of Puller (a leg wound sustained on Guadalcanal was giving him severe pain) and his men, Geiger conferred with Rupertus and some of his staff and after a bitter argument ordered Rupertus to replace the 1st Marines with the 321st RCT of the 81st Inf. Div., now on Angaur, and send Puller and his crippled unit back to Pavuvu. The 1st Marines by this time reported 1,749 casualties. One Marine later described the fighting in the Umurbrogol, which attests to the level to which the 1st Marines had deteriorated:

"I picked up the rifle of a dead Marine and I went up the hill; I remember no more than a few yards of scarred hillside, I didn't worry about death anymore, I had resigned from the human race. I crawled and scrambled forward and lay still without any feeling towards any human thing. In the next foxhole was a rifleman. He peered at me through red and painful eyes. I didn't care about him and he didn't care about me. As a fighting unit, the 1st Marines was finished. We were no longer human beings, I fired at anything that moved in front of me, friend or foe. I had no friends, I just wanted to kill."

SIDESHOWS ON ANGAUR AND ULITHI

The IIIAC Reserve for Operation Stalemate II was the 81st Inf. Div., to be used as necessary and then to assault Angaur with two of its three RCTs but only when the situation was "well in hand" on Peleliu. The

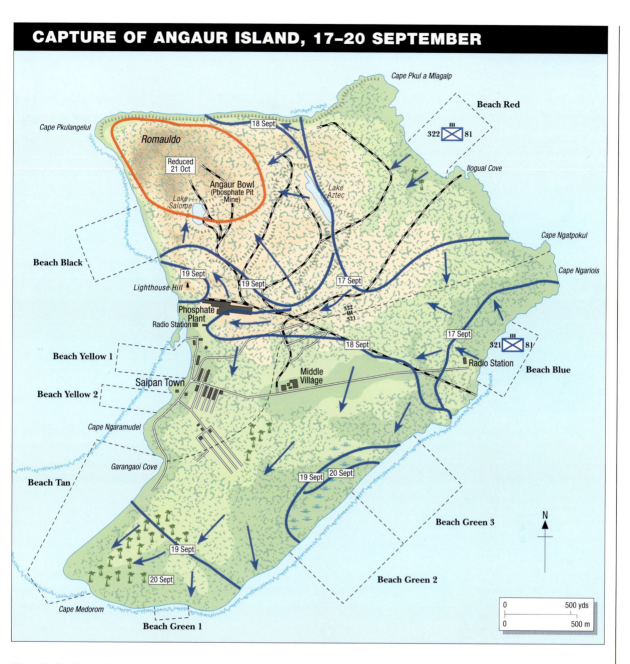

CAPTURE OF ANGAUR ISLAND, 17–20 SEPTEMBER

Cape Pkul a Mlagalp

Beach Red

Cape Pkulangelul

322 | 81

Romauldo

Ilogual Cove

Reduced
21 Oct

Angaur Bowl
(Phosphate Pit
Mine)

Lake
Aztec

18 Sept

Lake
Salome

Cape Ngatpokul

Beach Black

Cape Ngariois

19 Sept

19 Sept

17 Sept

Lighthouse Hill

Phosphate
Plant

322
321

Radio Station

17 Sept

18 Sept

321 | 81

Beach Yellow 1

Radio Station

Saipan Town

Middle
Village

Beach Blue

Beach Yellow 2

Cape Ngaramudel

Garangaoi Cove

19 Sept 20 Sept

N

Beach Tan

Beach Green 3

19 Sept

20 Sept

Beach Green 2

Cape Medorom

0   500 yds

0   500 m

Beach Green 1

81st Inf. Div. Command Post afloat was aboard the USS *Fremont* (APA-42).

On 16 September (D+1) 1st Mar. Div. commander, General Rupertus, gave the assurance that "Peleliu would be secured in a few more days" and so, on Rupertus' report, LtGen Geiger issued orders for the assault on Angaur to proceed. F-Day, the Angaur assault was set for 17 September (D+2 on Peleliu). F-Day was used to designate the Angaur assault to prevent confusion with Peleliu's D-Day. Likewise, G-Hour was used rather than H-Hour. Angaur Island lies 7 miles southwest of Peleliu. Major Goto Ushio of the 1st Battalion, 59th Infantry (Reinforced) detached from the 14th Division, would make his last stand with some 1,400 troops. He had divided the island into four defense sectors and a small central reserve.

The remnants of Col Chesty Puller's 1st Marines on their way out of the line having been relieved by elements of the 7th Marines. They were initially told this was only a brief respite for a few days, but it was clear the 1st Marines were a spent force and MajGen Geiger ordered them to return to their base on Pavuvu.

Major Goto had expected the Americans to land on the superb beaches on the southeast of the island, codenamed Beaches Green 1 and 2 by the Americans; and so it was here Goto constructed his most formidable coastal defenses of steel-reinforced concrete bunkers and blockhouses in addition to numerous antiboat gun emplacements, machine gun nests, and rifle pits. Goto also sowed numerous minefields along the 1,400-yard stretch of beach.

All this would be to no avail as reconnaissance missions over Angaur had spotted all this construction activity months earlier and so the American planners had rejected plans to use the Green Beaches as being too heavily fortified for an amphibious assault, choosing instead the less well-defended Beaches Red and Blue to the north and east.

As planned the 322nd RCT landed on Beach Red on the northeast coast and 321st RCT landed on Beach Blue on the upper southeast, both after a full pre-landing bombardment from the Navy, involving the battleship USS *Tennessee* (BB-43), one heavy cruiser and three light cruisers. In addition, 40 Dauntless dive-bombers from the aircraft carrier USS *Wasp* (CV-18) bombed and strafed the beaches and the areas immediately inland. As at Peleliu, rocket-firing LCI(G)s saturated the beach areas with 4.5in. rocket salvos in advance of the first assault waves boated in amtracs and preceded by armored LVT(A)s as initial tank support. Both RCTs encountered only small-scale resistance from small arms and mortars on the beaches and were soon pushing inland, although 321st RCT on Beach Blue initially met with some stiff resistance, coming under fire on both flanks from Japanese fortifications on Rockey Point on the left flank and from Cape Ngatpokul on the right. The 323rd RCT remained afloat and conducted a feint off Beach Green.

Soon after the push inland started, the "Wildcats" found themselves snarled up in dense scrub forests infested with Japanese machine guns and snipers. The advance was slow and costly but by nightfall both RCTs had reached their objective lines but were still separated by some 1,500 yards, so the RCTs both formed their own independent perimeter.

During the night, several Japanese counterattacks hit both RCTs causing the Americans to withdraw from some positions. 1/321 fell back some 75 yards in order to regroup and reorganize its lines, but all the Japanese attacks were eventually beaten off.

The second day, after a three-hour artillery bombardment with bombing and strafing sorties from Navy carrier planes, both RCTs advanced with tank support north and west and the right flank of the 321st RCT made contact with 322nd RCT, linking the two advances together. The 322nd RCT pushed west from Beach Red, making good time until they reached the center of the island and the high ground where Maj Goto had sited his final redoubt. By early afternoon, the 322nd had reached the phosphate plant just northeast of Saipan Town (the island's capital). During 322nd's advance, the 3rd Battalion came under "friendly fire" from carrier planes due to a mix-up over grid coordinates, resulting in 7 dead and 46 wounded – this did nothing for inter-service cooperation!

The 321st RCT advanced west from Beach Blue with 322nd RCT now on its right flank. The 321st pushed to the south, progressing well until

Tank dozer, a bulldozer blade fitted to the front of a Sherman tank, was a very useful and effective weapon at the disposal of the attacking soldiers and Marines on Peleliu. Here one fires on one of the many Japanese defenses after clearing itself a path to a position where it can get a better shot at the defending Japanese.

The 2.36in. M1A1 rocket launcher, or bazooka as it was better known, was a very useful weapon for tackling bunkers and cave defenses and was used extensively by both the Marine and Army units.

they came up against the formidable defenses of Beach Green, a series of mutually supporting fortifications covering some 1,500 yards, here 1/321 stopped and dug in for the night.

On the third day (19 September), after a night of many Japanese infiltrations and small scale counter-attacks, 321st RCT pushed on and succeeded in cutting the island in two. The 321st RCT assaulted the Beach Green defenses from inland and with the aid of tanks and support weapons they were able to reduce the fortifications one by one. This was due mainly to the fact that most of the fortifications' firing ports faced out to sea, in the direction of the anticipated invasion. In fact the 321st's attack came from their blind side to the rear, where the fortifications were not mutually supporting. The 321st then wheeled left and pushed down the southwest of the island, stopping just short of the shoreline by nightfall. By the end of the third day, there remained only two areas still in Japanese hands; the biggest and most formidable being in the northeast centered around Romauldo Hill, a series of coral ridges and outcrops even more rugged than, but not as large as, on Peleliu. With the situation reportedly well in hand on Peleliu and Angaur, the IIIAC Reserve, the 81st Inf. Div.'s third RCT, the 323rd, was sent on to its secondary target of Ulithi Island as planned.

On the fourth day the last remaining Japanese pockets of resistance in the south and around the Beach Green defenses were dispatched and 322nd RCT began reducing the Romauldo Pocket. It would take another four weeks of bitter hand-to-hand fighting before Maj Goto and his men, well armed with rifles, machine guns, and mortars, and dug well into the mass of caves and tunnels in the Romauldo Hills, were crushed, and then only with the extensive use of flamethrowers, grenades, and demolitions alongside the sheer determination of the "Wildcats." On 19 October, Maj Goto was killed during fighting for one

Marines survey one of the Japanese heavy gun positions still littered with the debris of the battle. Note the ample amounts of ammunition the Japanese defenders had and the 360° points of the compass painted on the revetment wall, this weapon being capable of all-round fire, although there is no sign of the gun itself.

of the many cave complexes and three days later the last of the Japanese defenses was reduced, finally bringing to an end organized resistance on Angaur – although Japanese stragglers would be encountered for many months to follow. On the same day, the 81st commander, MajGen Meuller, was contacted by IIIAC commander General Geiger, regarding the need for an RCT for immediate deployment to Peleliu. General Mueller replied that the 321st RCT would be available as soon as it could be reorganized and as such began transferring to Peleliu on 20 September. Angaur was declared secure at 1034hrs on 20 September by MajGen Mueller even though the 322nd RCT overran the last pocket in the hills on 21 October – a full month later.

Casualties for the 81st were comparatively light compared to those on Peleliu; 260 killed, 1,354 wounded, and 940 incapacitated for

Japanese hand-drawn artillery caught in the open on the east/west road have suffered the full wrath of Navy and Marine fighter-bombers. With total air superiority, the American air support made short work of any Japanese caught in the open.

non-combat reasons. The Japanese lost an estimated 1,338 killed and 59 taken prisoner.

A further sideshow was conducted 370 miles to the northeast. The 323rd RCT was dispatched on 19 September to secure Ulithi Atoll, a mission originally envisioned for the 321st RCT. On 17 September, F-Day on Angaur, it was decided to commit the Ulithi Landing Force. This necessitated re-embarking some units that had already landed on Angaur including the 906th Field Artillery Battalion. Landing on J-Day, 22 September, they found the atoll's airfield and seaplane base to be abandoned. Elements of 323rd RCT also searched Ngulu Atoll (16–17 October), Pulo Anna Island (20 November), Kayangel Atoll (28 November–1 December), and Faris Island (1–4 January 1945). Here 17 Japanese were discovered with eight killed, two taken prisoner, and three fleeing by boat. US losses were two killed and five wounded. A major advanced fleet anchorage was established at Ulithi along with a Marine airbase and a Navy seaplane base.

"A HORRIBLE PLACE"

On 23 September (D+8), Company G, 2nd Battalion secured the small unnamed and undefended island (later nicknamed "Carlson Island") north of Ngabad Island, completing the 5th Marines' original mission. A pontoon causeway was completed by Seabees on Beach Orange 3 on D+6 and this greatly expedited the unloading of supplies and equipment from Landing Ships, Tank (LST) as it bridged the reef impassable to the large beaching craft.

The Japanese attempted to reinforce the garrison on Peleliu on the night of 23/24 September (D+8/9). Barges had been sent on two occasions from Koror and Babelthuap and both times had been intercepted by the Americans, but Col Nakagawa did receive almost a battalion's (2nd Battalion, 15th Infantry) worth of fresh, if slightly mauled, troops. The need to secure northern Peleliu became more pressing than the elimination of defenses in the Umurbrogol Mountains to prevent further reinforcement landings.

The 81st Inf. Div.'s 321st RCT began arriving on 23 September from Angaur and began to relieve Puller's battered 1st Marines who were initially withdrawn to the south of the island to rest. The 321st RCT landed over the Orange Beaches task organized as follows:

321st Regimental Combat Team
321st Infantry
Company A, 306th Engineer Combat Battalion
  Detachment, HQ and Service Company, 306th Engineer Combat Battalion
Company A (Collecting), 306th Medical Battalion
Company D (Clearing) (– two platoons), 306th Medical Battalion
  Detachment, HQ Company, 306th Medical Battalion
154th Engineer Combat Battalion (– one company)
  Detachment, HQ and Service Company, 1138th Engineer Combat Group
Detachment, 592d Joint Assault Signal Company
Detachment, 481st Transportation Corps Amphibious Truck Company (DUKW)
Company B, 726th Amphibian Tractor Battalion
  Detachment, HQ and Service Company, 726th Amphibian Tractor Battalion
Company A, 710th Tank Battalion
  Provisional 81mm Mortar Platoon, 710th Tank Battalion
Company D, 88th Chemical Battalion (Motorized) (4.2in. mortar)
Detachment, Provisional Graves Registration Company, 81st Inf. Div.
Detachment, 81st Signal Company
Detachment, 81st Quartermaster Company
Detachment, 81st Ordnance Light Maintenance Company
Detachment, Translator-Interpreter Team A, HQ Company, Central Pacific Area

On 24 September (D+9) the 321st RCT began to drive north up the peninsula. The plan was for 321st RCT to push past the Umurbrogol Pocket with the 5th Marines, passing through 321st RCT and on into northern Peleliu, with the 7th Marines taking over the 1st Marines' positions. The West Road running up the peninsula would be 321st's main route for the drive north, but the Japanese still held the coral knobs and ridges that dominated the road, and brought anything on the road under murderous fire.

The terrain to the east side of the road made it impossible to use tanks or any other vehicle, thus forcing the use of infantry with no close support, climbing and clambering over coral and ridges to protect the

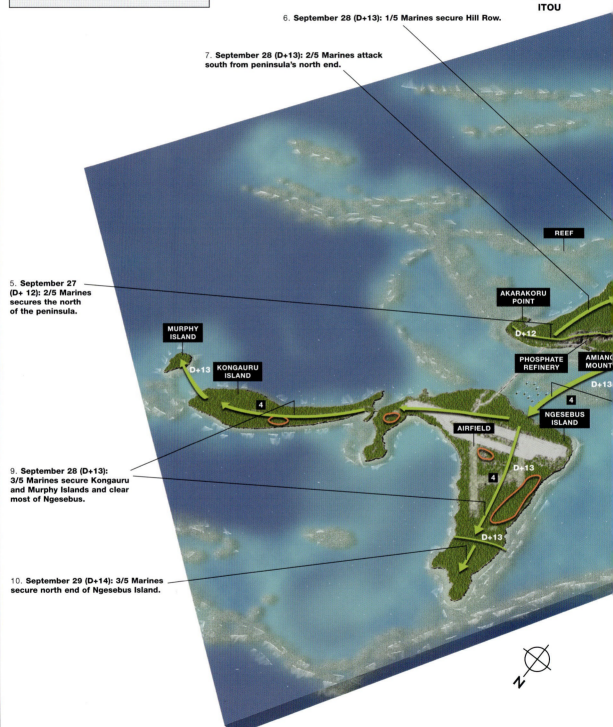

US FORCES
1 5th Marines
2 1st Battalion, 5th Marines
3 2nd Battalion, 5th Marines
4 3rd Battalion, 5th Marines
5 2nd and 3rd Battalions, 321st Infantry Regiment

Base
Force Peleliu
ITOU

6. **September 28 (D+13): 1/5 Marines secure Hill Row.**

7. **September 28 (D+13): 2/5 Marines attack south from peninsula's north end.**

5. **September 27 (D+ 12): 2/5 Marines secures the north of the peninsula.**

REEF

AKARAKORU POINT

D+12

MURPHY ISLAND

D+13

KONGAURU ISLAND

4

PHOSPHATE REFINERY

AMIANG **MOUNT**

D+13

4

NGESEBUS ISLAND

AIRFIELD

9. **September 28 (D+13): 3/5 Marines secure Kongauru and Murphy Islands and clear most of Ngesebus.**

D+13

4

10. **September 29 (D+14): 3/5 Marines secure north end of Ngesebus Island.**

D+13

N

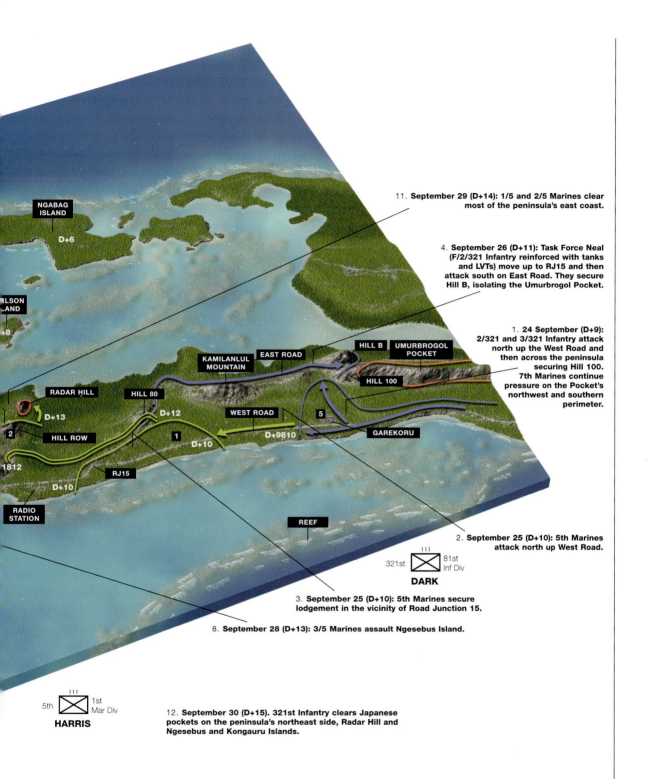

NGABAG ISLAND
D+6

RLSON AND
+8

11. **September 29 (D+14): 1/5 and 2/5 Marines clear most of the peninsula's east coast.**

4. **September 26 (D+11): Task Force Neal (F/2/321 Infantry reinforced with tanks and LVTs) move up to RJ15 and then attack south on East Road. They secure Hill B, isolating the Umurbrogol Pocket.**

1. **24 September (D+9): 2/321 and 3/321 Infantry attack north up the West Road and then across the peninsula securing Hill 100. 7th Marines continue pressure on the Pocket's northwest and southern perimeter.**

HILL B   UMURBROGOL POCKET

KAMILANLUL MOUNTAIN   EAST ROAD

HILL 100

RADAR HILL   HILL 80

WEST ROAD   5

D+13   D+12

2   HILL ROW   1   D+10   D+9810   GAREKORU

1812

RJ15   D+10

RADIO STATION

REEF

2. **September 25 (D+10): 5th Marines attack north up West Road.**

321st ⊠ 81st Inf Div
DARK

3. **September 25 (D+10): 5th Marines secure lodgement in the vicinity of Road Junction 15.**

8. **September 28 (D+13): 3/5 Marines assault Ngesebus Island.**

5th ⊠ 1st Mar Div
HARRIS

12. **September 30 (D+15). 321st Infantry clears Japanese pockets on the peninsula's northeast side, Radar Hill and Ngesebus and Kongauru Islands.**

SECURING THE NORTH

24–29 September (D+9 to D+14), viewed from the northwest showing operations to secure the north end of Peleliu, Ngesebus and Kongauru Islands.

right flank. Once these ridges were taken, vehicles could use the West
Road to support and supply the advance.

The 321st had relieved the 3/1 Marines that had been tied to 3/7 on
the right flank, orders required 3/7 to advance behind 2/321 along the
high ground as the soldiers pushed northeast. However, 3/7 were soon
outpaced by 2/321 on the flat ground but instead of attacking the ridges
2/321 units abandoned them for the road, reporting 3/7 were not
keeping up with them. Colonel Hanneken ordered 3/7 to capture the
ridges abandoned by 2/321, which they did at some cost – another
setback in Army–Marine relations! The 321st pushed on and by D+10
the 5th Marines were able to pass through them for the final drive at
the ruins of Garekoru Village. On the afternoon of D+10 1/5 seized
the destroyed radio station complex to the north of Garekoru with
3/5 taking high ground on 1/5's right. Japanese defenses were as
formidable as any on Peleliu, but were reduced by tanks, flamethrowers,
and demolition charges, many of the defending unit being poorly
trained Navy construction personnel.

Four steep-sided limestone hills running east–west across the
northeastern peninsula were attacked on D+11. These had been dubbed
Hills 1, 2, and 3 and Radar Hill, known as "Hill Row," and were actually
the southern arm of Amiangal Ridge. They were defended by some
1,500 infantrymen, artillerymen, and naval construction troops plus
reinforcements from Koror. As the right progressed 2/5 side-stepped to
the west and pushed on to the north, leaving 1/5 to continue the assault
and by nightfall had taken the southern end of the final ridge. What 2/5
did not know was that they were facing the most comprehensive cave
system on Peleliu which was the underground home of the Japanese
naval construction units who were, luckily for the Marines, better miners
than infantrymen.

Fighting continued all day D+11 and D+12 with several small scale
counterattacks during the night but by the end of D+12 2/5 had secured
the northern shore (Akarakoro Point) though if the Marines held the
area above ground, the Japanese still held it underground! It would take
weeks for the Marines to finally quash all resistance on Akarakoro Point,
then only by blasting closed all the tunnel entrances, sealing the
Japanese defenders inside to their fate. The Marines were amazed

several weeks later to witness the Japanese Navy survivors digging their way out to the surface.

2/5 then turned around and attacked south in support of 1/5, still slogging away at the four rocky hills of Hill Row. After two days of bitter fighting the Marines blasted and burned their way to the tops of Hill Row, most of the Japanese defenders being sealed in their caves and left to their own devices, but by D+14 all but the Umurbrogol Pocket had been taken.

Whilst their comrades of 1/5 and 2/5 battled it out on Hill Row, Marines of 3/5 prepared for an amphibious assault on Ngesebus and Kongauru Islands, some 300 yards off Akarakora Point. Ngesebus Island was L-shaped and around 2,500 yards long. Much smaller Kongauru Island lay off its northeastern tip. Ngesebus was surrounded by a coral reef estimated to be 4ft deep and had been connected to mainland Peleliu by a wooden causeway, this having been partially destroyed during the preliminary bombardment. Ngesebus Island had been sited as one of the prime targets on Peleliu during the planning stages due to the presence of a secondary airfield, albeit a smaller fighter strip. Now, with the campaign in full swing and Japanese airpower on Peleliu destroyed, a much greater priority for the Americans was to prevent the use of Ngesebus and Kongauru Islands as a staging area for Japanese reinforcements sent by General Inoue from Koror and Babelthuap.

The landing planned by Col Harris and LtCol Walt was a textbook operation. Major Gustafason, 3/5, was to land on the shores of Ngesebus after a massive pre-landing naval bombardment from the battleship USS *Mississippi* (BB-41), the cruisers *Denver* (CL-58) and *Columbus* (CA-74), and land-based artillery. Marine Corsair fighter-bombers from VMF-114 operating from Peleliu Airfield would provide air cover. Notably, this was the first time a US Marine amphibious landing had been supported entirely by Marine aviation. Major General Rupertus was so supremely confident in the success of the wholly Marine operation that (reminiscent of Civil War Yankee generals at the first battle of Bull Run in 1861) he invited along a party of dignitaries including Admiral Oldendorf, who had already "run out of target" weeks before, to witness the proceedings from the comfort and safety of their armor-plated podiums. 1/7 stood by in reserve. 3/5 was supported by a company of LVTs to carry the assault troops, an armored LVT(A) company, and a company of waterproofed

Fully waterproofed Sherman tanks of the 1st Marine Tank Battalion preceded by a tank-dozer cross the shallow water between Peleliu and Ngesebus island in support of 3/5. Unfortunately the waterproofing on three of the Shermans proved inadequate and they were swamped, having to be recovered later. In the background can be seen the wooden causeway between Ngesebus and Peleliu partially destroyed in the pre-invasion bombardment.

REDUCING THE UMURBROGOL POCKET (pages 54–55)
The incredibly chaotic and broken terrain of the Umurbrogol
Pocket proved to be some of the most difficult ground fought
over during the entire Pacific war. Countless caves, ravines,
gorges, crevasses, and sinkholes honeycombed the coral and
limestone hills and ridges of the Umurbrogol Mountains.
Flamethrowers, satchel charges, fragmentation grenades, and
rocket launchers ("Zippos, corkscrews, pineapples, and
bazookas") were required to reduce strongpoints through
close assault. Most vegetation had been blasted away and
many of the mutually supporting Japanese positions were on
inaccessible terrain lacking covered approaches. Often the
Marines were forced to carry filled sandbags from the
beaches and shove them into protective piles (1) with poles in
order to obtain suitable firing positions. A new weapon tested
on Peleliu was the 60mm T20 shoulder-fired mortar (2). It
proved to be too heavy, parts broke easily, and the recoil too
debilitating, with gunners having to be replaced after firing
three or four rounds. Its development had been one of several
attempts to provide a mortar with capabilities similar to the
Japanese 50mm Type 89 (1929) heavy grenade discharger
or "knee mortar," as well as provide a weapon capable of
direct-fire to attack pillboxes. The 2.36in. M1A1 "bazooka"
rocket launcher was widely used at this time and proved to
be a much more effective, reliable, and lighter weapon
than the T20 mortar. The T20 relied on its high explosive
projectile (3) being fired directly though a pillbox firing slit
or cave entrance to be effective. It had no penetration effect.
The bazooka's high explosive antitank shaped-charge
warhead could penetrate concrete, rock, timber, and
sandbag-constructed pillboxes and would be almost as
effective if firing through a firing port. A unique unit
attached to the 1st Mar. Div. was the US Navy Flamethrower
Detachment. It was formed in the States in May 1944 and
attached as a test unit to the 1st Mar. Div. in early June.
Its single Navy officer and two petty officers trained Marine
crewman to man LVT(4) amtracs fitted with Canadian-made
Ronson Mk 1 flameguns (4). Also known as the "Q" flame unit,
the flameguns had a range of 75 yards with unthickened fuel
and 150 yards with thickened fuel. This made the flame
amtracs extremely valuable for burning out caves and
pillboxes in the Umurbrogol Mountains. It could reach enemy
positions out of range of man-packed M1A1 flamethrowers,
which had a range of only 40–50 yards. The flame amtracs
carried 200 gallons of fuel allowing a flame duration of
55 seconds with unthickened fuel and 80 seconds with
thickened. They were normally fired in 3–5-second bursts.
Unthickened fuel was straight gasoline while thickened fuel
consisted of gasoline mixed with napalm powder or bunker C
Navy fuel oil and diesel fuel. The detachment initially had six
flame amtracs with a two-amtrac section attached to each
Marine regiment. Each section was backed by a support
amtrac carrying flame fuel, bottles of compressed carbon
dioxide (the flame fuel's propellant), and a pressure fuel
transfer pump. Later a third flame amtrac was added to each
section using spare flameguns. The detachment remained in
support of the 81st Inf. Div. after the Marines departed.
(Howard Gerrard)

Sherman tanks supported by UDT 6. The assault got ashore by 0930hrs with no casualties, although the "waterproofing" on the first three Sherman tanks proved inadequate and they were swamped. The Marines proceeded to knock out all beach defenses before turning their attention inland. Ngesebus is mainly flat, covered by scrub, although to the west of the island there was an area of high ground made up of coral ridges and sink holes, reminiscent of mainland Peleliu and now familiar to the Marines. This area was where the Japanese made their main defense line. These defenses though were not mutually supporting like those in the Umurbrogol and so, with the support of tanks and armored LVTs, by the end of the day (D+13) 3/5 had overrun most of the opposition. L/3/5 supported by tanks pushed east, parallel to and past the airstrip to the eastern tip of Ngesebus and across to Kongauru Island while K/3/5 assaulted the high ground and the main Japanese defenses in the west.

D+14 (29 September) was spent mopping up in the western high ground and by 1500hrs Ngesebus and Kongauru were declared secure. Colonel Nakagawa had lost 463 first-rate troops at a cost to the Americans of 15 dead and 33 wounded and all in just 36 hours. Although small pockets of resistance on the islands remained, more importantly Peleliu was now cut off from reinforcement from the rest of the Japanese forces in the Palaus. 3/5 turned the islands over to 2/321 and went into divisional reserve for a well-earned rest. The 321st would have to complete the clearing of these islands and establish security outposts. On 30 September (D+15) MajGen Rupertus declared that "organized resistance has ended on Ngesebus and all of northern Peleliu has been secured," a statement that brought many a derogatory comment from Marines and soldiers still fighting and dying on and around the north of Peleliu and who would be for many more weeks to come.

On 24 September the Kossol Passage north of Babelthuap was swept of mines and three days later a fleet resupply anchorage was in operation there to support the continued assault.

"THE POCKET"

All of Peleliu but the Umurbrogol Mountains was now largely in American hands and the assault on the Japanese defenses in the Umurbrogol Pocket now took on the air of a Medieval siege.

With the attacks from the north by 2/321 and 3/321 the encirclement of the Pocket was complete whilst the 7th Marines continued to press from the south and west. The Pocket was now down to 1,000 yards by 500 yards in size, not much bigger than ten football fields.

Hill B, which had stalled 321's attack, was finally reduced on D+11, allowing 321 to continue the assault on the Pocket from the north. Progress was limited but it did allow the Americans to consolidate their hold on the north side of the Pocket.

On D+14 the 7th Marines were ordered to relieve 2/321 and 3/321 in the north but in order to release 2/7 and 3/7 from their holding position on the west of the Pocket the 1st Division command stripped hundreds of men from support units to form two composite groups to secure the north side of the Pocket. They were disbanded on 16 October when the Pocket was compressed further.

Here a flame-thrower gives welcome support to troops attacking a Japanese cave position. Six Navy Mk. 1 flame-throwers were fitted to amtracs for Peleliu and although very effective, the limited maneuverability of the LVT(4) (they were slow and unwieldy out of water) was a problem. The flame-throwers were later fitted to medium tanks, which proved far more effective.

At the same time as these composite units were being thrown together, MajGen Rupertus made a less than sound decision by ordering the 1st Tank Battalion, which still had at least a dozen serviceable Sherman tanks in the field, to return with the 1st Marines to Pavuvu. This astounded other members of his staff with the assistant division commander, BrigGen Oliver P. Smith, later calling it "a bad mistake, the tanks were sorely missed when heavy mobile firepower was so important."

As if the situation was not delicate enough, nature decided to remind mankind who was in charge by sending down a typhoon, which lasted for three days making it impossible for the Americans to land rations, fuel, and ammunition. Shortages soon developed and transport planes braved the weather to deliver tons of much needed supplies. At least the typhoon did allow the temperature to drop from its usual 110°F to 80°F during the day, but this was soon offset by the dust turning to mud and making vehicle and foot movement difficult in most areas.

1/7 and 3/7 relieved the 321st on D+14 and on D+15 renewed the assault southwards, succeeding in partially taking "Boyd Ridge" and its southern extension Hill 100 (sometimes referred to as Popes Ridge or Walt Ridge) though Japanese defenders remained in caves on the western slopes.

On D+18 the 7th Marines were reinforced by 3/5 (back from Ngesebus) and planned a four-battalion attack from the north and south: the 1/7 and 3/7 from the north and 2/7 from the south with 3/5 making a diversionary attack to the west into "Horseshoe Canyon" and "Five Sisters." After bitter fighting and heavy casualties the attack secured its objectives with the exception of Five Sisters. Although four out of five "Sisters" were scaled by 3/5 their position became untenable and they had to abandon their gains. On D+18 the assault on Five Sisters was repeated, unfortunately with the same result as the day before! It was also on D+18 (3 October) that the 1st Mar. Div. lost its highest ranking officer killed in action on Peleliu, when Colonel Joseph F. Hankins, Commanding Officer, Division Headquarters Battalion, was killed on the West Road at a point affectionately known as "Dead Man's Curve." A mixed convoy of Army and Marine trucks had been brought to a standstill by Japanese rifle and

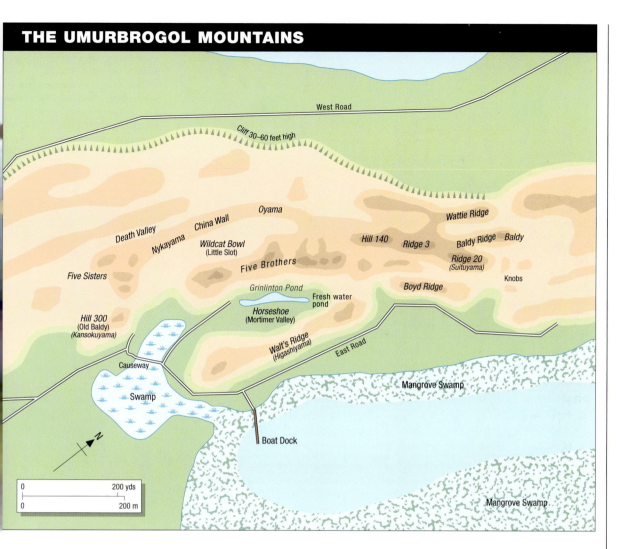

machine gun fire. In an effort to get the convoy moving again, Hankins was seen striding down the center of the road cursing at the drivers to get moving, showing a total disregard for his own safety, and was cut down by a hail of machine gun fire and died instantly.

By now the 7th Marines had been in the Umurbrogol for two weeks. The 7th Marines landed on D-Day with 3,217 men, of whom 1,486 were now dead, wounded, or missing. They had sustained 46 per cent casualties in a little under three weeks of fighting and their four battalions, including the attached 3/5, were now close to company-strength. General Geiger suggested to Gen Rupertus that he should relieve the 7th Marines. Reluctantly he did, reporting to General Geiger once again that it would be all over "in a few more days." Rupertus turned to his only remaining regiment, the 5th Marines.

With the introduction of the 5th Marines to the assault on the pocket, Col Harris implemented two new "policies," which would remain in place until the end of the fighting.

First, the attack on the pocket would be made exclusively from the north, which offered best opportunity to chip away at the many ridges one at a time. Second, aerial reconnaissance conducted by Col Harris

Tanks and infantry of 81st Infantry Division move into the Horseshoe in the Umurbrogol pocket. On the left is " Five brothers," the small pond barely seen above the large sinkhole in the foreground was the only source of fresh water for the Japanese and many were kiilled attempting to canteens under cover of darkness.

during the first week on Peleliu showed him how formidable the Umurbrogol was. Now stripped of overlaying vegetation the numerous steep ridges, hills, sinkholes, gorges, and caves, to say nothing of the formidable Japanese defenses, became apparent, and it would clearly only be taken using siege tactics. He intended to "be lavish with ammunition and stingy with men's lives."

2/5 relieved 3/7 on D+20, but did nothing other than reconnoiter positions. Bulldozers were brought up to clear entrances to the many canyons to the north allowing flamethrower-equipped LVTs and tanks to operate. Also, artillery was positioned on the West Road to provide pointblank fire into west-facing cliffs. On D+22 a tank sortie went into the Horseshoe but this time only to shell identified targets and then withdraw.

These tactics continued for the next six days, slowly reducing the Pocket. The capture of Hill 140 allowed a 75mm pack howitzer to be manhandled up into position, and sand-bagged in place (filled sandbags being hauled up from the beaches) to fire directly into the mouths of larger caves, one of which was pouring murderous fire down onto the attackers.

On D+27 3/5 was called to relieve 2/5 but the relief suffered from heavy sniper fire and small-scale counterattacks from Nakagawa's men that resulted in more losses to the Marines. The relief was complete by D+28, however, with 3/5 takingover where 2/5 had finished.

3/5 continued to push from the north using their siege tactics and, with similar efforts from what was left of 1/7 in the south, the Pocket had been reduced to an area some 800 yards long by 500 yards wide. Nakagawa reported to Koror by radio that he was down to fewer than 700 effective troops.

Still Rupertus insisted the Pocket could be taken solely by his Marines "in a few days," turning down once again the assistance of Mueller's 81st Infantry Division. Lieutenant General Geiger suggested to

Rupertus that first the 5th then the 7th Marines be relieved by 321st RCT, but once again Rupertus replied that his Marines would "very shortly" subdue the Pocket. However, events overtook Rupertus; first the 81st detached RCT – the 323rd – arrived from Ulithi, then Admiral Wilkinson, the overall commander at Peleliu, was ordered to return to Hawaii and Admiral Fort to replace him. Upon taking command, Admiral Fort sent a communiqué stating Peleliu had been secured, meaning the airfield was usable, much to the amazement of the men still fighting there, and that the "Assault Phase" of Operation Stalemate II was complete. Lieutenant General Geiger was therefore directed to relieve the 1st Mar. Div. and turn the islands over to the 81st Inf. Div. to mop-up and garrison. The 1st Mar. Div. was to return to Pavuvu.

During D+31/32, the 321st RCT relieved the 5th Marines, 1/7 still battling away in the Pocket until they in turn were relieved by 1/323, newly arrived from Ulithi on D+32. The 81st Inf. Div. designated the Pocket the Central Combat Zone. Some Marine units remained to support the Army including detachments of the 1st Amphibian Tractor, 3rd Armored Amphibian Tractor, and 1st Medical Battalions plus the 8th 155mm Gun and 12th Defense Battalions.

On 30 October Gen Geiger officially handed over command of Peleliu to MajGen Mueller. It took the 81st Inf. Div. nearly six weeks, using essentially the same siege tactics as the Marines, to reduce the Pocket.

By now the Japanese defenses in the Pocket measured some 800yds by 400yds, consisting of individual defenses around the areas of Baldy, Hill 140, Five Brothers, Five Sisters, and the China Wall. As the attack was renewed Bulldozers cleared the way for tanks and flame-throwing LVTs and Marine aircraft from VMF-114 dropped hundreds of bombs and napalm canisters in low-level sorties. The pilots were over their targets so soon after take-off from Peleliu airstrip that they did not have time to retract their undercarriage.

Setting out from Kongauru Island in early October, 2/321 cleared the many small Northern Islands between Peleliu and Koror including Garakayo, Bairakaseru, Garyo, Ngemelis, Arimasuku, and others.

Aerial view of the Umurbrogol Mountains taken after Peleliu had been secured. At top left and bottom right are the main coast roads, which ran the whole length of the island. This photo shows clearly the numerous ridges, valleys and sinkholes, now devoid of any vegetation, which made up mountains.

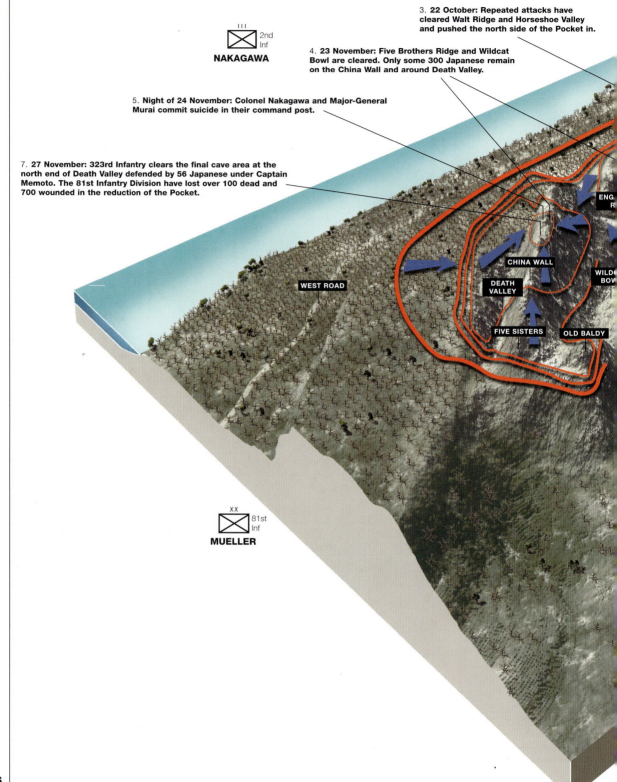

3. 22 October: Repeated attacks have cleared Walt Ridge and Horseshoe Valley and pushed the north side of the Pocket in.

4. 23 November: Five Brothers Ridge and Wildcat Bowl are cleared. Only some 300 Japanese remain on the China Wall and around Death Valley.

5. Night of 24 November: Colonel Nakagawa and Major-General Murai commit suicide in their command post.

7. 27 November: 323rd Infantry clears the final cave area at the north end of Death Valley defended by 56 Japanese under Captain Memoto. The 81st Infantry Division have lost over 100 dead and 700 wounded in the reduction of the Pocket.

2nd
Inf
NAKAGAWA

WEST ROAD

CHINA WALL

DEATH
VALLEY

ENG.
R

WILD
BOW

FIVE SISTERS

OLD BALDY

81st
Inf
MUELLER

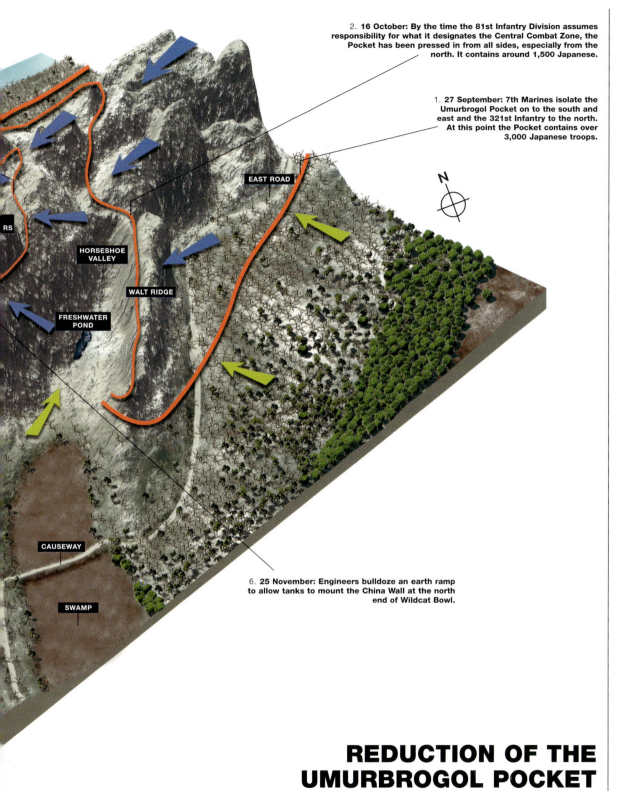

2. **16 October:** By the time the 81st Infantry Division assumes responsibility for what it designates the Central Combat Zone, the Pocket has been pressed in from all sides, especially from the north. It contains around 1,500 Japanese.

1. **27 September:** 7th Marines isolate the Umurbrogol Pocket on to the south and east and the 321st Infantry to the north. At this point the Pocket contains over 3,000 Japanese troops.

EAST ROAD

RS

HORSESHOE VALLEY

WALT RIDGE

FRESHWATER POND

CAUSEWAY

SWAMP

6. **25 November:** Engineers bulldoze an earth ramp to allow tanks to mount the China Wall at the north end of Wildcat Bowl.

REDUCTION OF THE UMURBROGOL POCKET

27 September–27 November, viewed from the south. Countless attacks were made on the pocket from all directions by a stream of constantly rotating units between 27 September, when it was isolated, and its fall on 27 November.

Security outposts were established on Garakayo, Ngesebus, Murphy, Carlson, Ngargersiul, and Ngabad Islands to prevent reinforcement from the north. On 20 October the Advance Headquarters, 81st Inf. Div. activated Ground Defense Headquarters. These islands as well as Peleliu's northeast peninsula north of the Central Combat Zone, were designated the Northern Defense Sector. The bulk of Peleliu south and east of the Central Combat Zone was designated the Southern Defense Sector. Outposts were established on other small islands further to the north in mid-November.

General Mueller resumed the assault on the Pocket, with 2/321 moving south from Hill 140 to attack the first of Five Brothers. They came under the usual hail of fire from the Japanese and were forced to retire. Further attacks met with the same results. It finally took a series of assaults by 2/321, with the aid of artillery and VMF-114 Corsairs, to finally take Brothers 1, 2, and 3. To the east 3/321 entered the "Horseshoe" with tanks and flame-throwing LVTs to blast and burn the cave defenses along the east side of Five Brothers.

The assault on the Horseshoe continued, the 321st finally being relieved by the returning 323rd. The 323rd commander, Col Arthur Watson, renewed the attacks to the south, 2/323 taking Hill 30 and Five Sisters and 3/323 beginning the assault on the China Wall. Unbeknownst to the Americans, they were within yards of Nakagawa's command post.

On 17 November, during a Japanese night-time infiltration, LtCol Raymond Gates, 323rd commanding officer, was killed by a sniper. He was the 81st Inf. Div.'s highest-ranking officer to be killed on Peleliu. The end on Peleliu was now only days away, Wildcat Bowl and Death Valley were in the hands of the Americans and Five Brothers was finally taken on 23 November, the last remaining Japanese defenders including Nakagawa and Murai were holed up in the China Wall defenses. Army engineers constructed a ramp using armored bulldozers near the north end of Wildcat Bowl enabling tanks and flame-throwing LVTs to fire directly onto the last Japanese defenses now only a couple of hundred square yards in area and being constantly assaulted from all directions.

On D+70 Col Nakagawa sent his final message to his superiors on Koror. He advised them he had burned the 2nd Infantry's colors and had split his last 56 men into 17 groups with orders to "attack the enemy everywhere." During the night of D+70/71, 25 Japanese were killed attempting infiltrations and, the following morning, a captured soldier confirmed that Col Nakagawa, along with MajGen Murai, had both committed ritual suicide in their command post.

Mid-morning on 27 November (D+73), units from the north and south met face-to-face near what turned out later to be Nakagawa's last command post. 323rd's Col Arthur Watson reported to General Mueller that the operation was over, although the reduction of small pockets continued for months and individuals and small groups of Japanese would turn up from time to time for years to come.

AFTERMATH

With the operation over there was time to reflect on the battle and evaluate the human cost. The Marines lost 1,050 killed in action, 250 died of wounds, 5,450 wounded, and 36 missing. Total casualties by regiment were: 1st Marines – 1,749, 5th Marines – 1,378, and 7th Marines – 1,497. The 81st Inf. Div. casualties on Peleliu were 1,393, of whom 208 were killed in action. A further 260 were killed and 1,354 wounded on Angaur. Japanese dead on Peleliu were an estimated at 10,900 including those lost at sea in reinforcement attempts and raids. Only 202 prisoners were taken; of these only 19 were Japanese, the remainder being Korean and Okinawan laborers. Virtually the entire 1,400-man garrison of Angaur was wiped out with only 59 prisoners being taken.

One aspect of the battle for Peleliu always mystified the American military, and that was the role played by MajGen Murai in the defense of the island. Captured orders examined after the battle, along with the interrogation of prisoners of war, indicated that the island commander was Col Nakagawa and that General Murai was there as a mere adviser. This appeared a most unusual situation, having a general as adviser to a colonel, particularly considering how strict the Japanese military code was. In addition the garrison on Peleliu was above the level of that usually commanded by a colonel.

In March 1950, General Inoue, who had survived the war and was on Guam in a US Navy prison, was interviewed by LtCol Worden, USMC. Inoue's testimony, and a report from the Japanese Ministry of Foreign Affairs, both confirmed General Murai was definitely on Peleliu during

Not all the Japanese defenders were quite ready to join their ancestors. Here five of the 200-plus prisoners of war taken on Peleliu are escorted to the rear by Military Police.

Marine Corsairs drop napalm onto Japanese defenses in the Umurbrogol. The time between take-off from the Peleliu airstrip and their target was so short that the pilots did not even have time to raise their undercarriage.

the battle and that both he and Col Nakagawa were promoted by special promotion on 31 December 1944, the day that both their deaths were accepted by the Japanese high command.

Peleliu was garrisoned for the next few months by units of the 81st Inf. Div. (321st RCT), also by Navy "Seabees" and Marine aviation units as well as the Marine 3rd Base Headquarters Battalion.

Although the fighting was officially over and Peleliu declared secure, groups and individual Japanese troops still remained in isolated pockets and caves, mainly in the north of the island and the Umurbrogol mountains. For months afterwards, the Army units left to garrison the island were flushing out stragglers and sealing up caves. Three months after the fighting in the Umurbrogol Pocket was over, the huge tunnel complex was still occupied by a handful of Japanese Navy and Army troops. After several attempts by the Americans to persuade them to surrender – to no avail – the entrances were blasted closed. To everyone's amazement, in February 1945, five surviving Japanese managed to dig their way out to the surface, only to be captured. Marine aircraft began arriving soon after D-Day on Peleliu: VMF-114, VMF-121, VMF-122, VMTB-134, VMF(N)-541, and VMR-952.

Also based on Peleliu after its fall were two Navy sea search units. Patrols from these units would discover the survivors from the USS *Indianapolis* (CA-35), the ill-fated ship that delivered elements of the atomic bomb to Tinian and, after departing Guam en route to Leyte, was sunk by the Japanese submarine I-58.

On 18 January 1945, totally out of the blue, Japanese troops from Babelthuap landed on Beaches Purple and White. After a brief struggle between them and the garrison forces, 71 Japanese lay dead and two had been captured.

The Kossol Passage north of Babelthuap, still occupied by the Japanese, remained in use as a fleet anchorage and, in conjunction with Ulithi, supported operations in the Philippines.

The 81st Inf. Div. remained on Peleliu and Angaur mopping up, clearing the battlefield of mounds of damaged equipment and materiel, guarding against possible seaborne raids from the north, and touring the battlefield until it departed between 6 December 1944 and 8 February 1945 sailing for New Caledonia where it would prepare for the assault on Okinawa in April 1945. The 1st Mar. Div. would fight there as well.

Years after the end of World War II, rumors persisted on Peleliu about surviving Japanese soldiers still hiding out in the mountains and swamps; eventually 120 Marines were sent to the island to search for survivors who were said to be preparing to attack Navy dependent housing. After several attempts to coax them out to surrender failed, a Japanese admiral was brought to Peleliu to convince the survivors that the war was over and it was acceptable to give themselves up with honor. Eventually on 22 April 1947, a lieutenant emerged along with 26 bedraggled 2nd Infantry soldiers and eight 45th Guard Force sailors – their battle for Peleliu was finally over. This was the last official surrender of World War II

Angaur was occupied by Navy Seabees, who started work constructing a 7,000ft airfield for the Army Air Forces, even before the island was secured, from which initially Marine aircraft wings flew sorties in support of the fighting still raging on Peleliu . It was later used by the 494th Heavy Bombardment Group which flew B-24 Liberators in support of US troops fighting in the Philippines. Raids were also flown against Koror and Babelthuap still occupied by General Inoue. The Navy established a small boat-repair facility on the island.

Whether Peleliu needed taking or not remains a subject of some deliberation by Generals and historians alike, but some facts are clear:
1. MacArthur's flank was secured for his return to the Philippines and the danger of Japanese air strikes or troop reinforcements from the Palaus was removed. This danger though was minimal as all Japanese aircraft in the Palaus had been destroyed and few of the Japanese barges were capable of the 700-mile open-sea trip to the Philippines.
2. Several thousand first-rate Japanese troops had been eliminated and the remaining troops in the Western Carolines could be contained by air and sea operations originating from the new American airbases on Peleliu and Angaur.
3. The change in Japanese tactics served as an early warning to the Allies of what to expect in the forthcoming operations on the Japanese homeland. This made the 1st Mar. Div. and 81st Inf. Div. two of the divisions best prepared for the coming battle on Okinawa.

Of the 1st Mar. Div.'s commanders, General Rupertus was relieved of his command and instead given command of the Marine Corps Schools back in the United States. He was awarded the Distinguished Service Medal in an action considered by many taken to keep him quiet. General Rupertus died of a heart attack at the Washington Navy Yard on 24 March 1945. He was 55 years old.

Colonels Puller, Harris, and Hanneken were all returned to the US for a long-overdue rest. The atomic bombs would be dropped on Hiroshima and Nagasaki before they received their next commands. Chesty Puller would go on to become the most decorated Marine in the history of the US Marine Corps.

THE BATTLEFIELD TODAY

Now the Republic of Palau, the former Palau Islands rank amongst the finest holiday destinations in the Pacific, especially if your interests are white sandy beaches and underwater exploration. There is now even a bridge connecting the former Japanese garrisoned islands of Koror and Babelthuap, funded by the Japanese Government and built by the Kajima Corporation. Built to foster good relations between Palau and Japan, the bridge was opened with great ceremony on 11 January 2002.

Today Peleliu lies largely forgotten, the scars of war overgrown by a dense carpet of tropical vegetation, but a closer inspection reveals an abundance of relics testifying to the battle and the occupation by the garrison troops afterwards.

US Marine Corps monument to the 1st Marine Division (Reinforced) on Peleliu. The 1st Mar. Div. was awarded the Presidential Unit Citation "for extraordinary heroism in action against enemy Japanese forces at Peleliu and Ngesebus from September 15 to 29 1944". (Eric Mailander)

Until the 1980s, visitors to the Palaus consisted mainly of Japanese veterans and relatives on nostalgia trips and very few Americans returned. However, the Palau Islands today boast some of the finest underwater diving locations anywhere in the world and, as such, many luxury hotels and complexes have appeared, mainly on Koror, as more and more people travel to the Palaus to experience the wonders of nature.

Also, from Koror, World War II historical battlefield tours are available to Peleliu and Angaur. Modern civilization is slowly coming to Peleliu, with electricity, television and many other trappings of today's rapidly developing world. Communication with the other islands in the Palaus is maintained both by boat and light aircraft, and young villagers conduct tours taking in many of the sites of the battle. In September 1999, a group of Marine Corps veterans of the battle for Peleliu, their sons and a few history buffs, returned to the island for the 55th anniversary of the battle. The beaches and the old Japanese airstrip are readily accessible and many relics, from bullets to LVTs, litter the battlefield. However, to view the sites up in the Umurbrogol Pocket, the visitor needs a stout pair of climbing boots and an even stouter heart, as the jungle has reclaimed many of the places that were so stark and barren all those years ago. Many of the caves, including Nakagawa's last command post, remain, and the efforts required to seek them out can be rewarding.

Tours of the villages also show many reminders of the battle, with small collections of artifacts and vehicles being displayed, although caution must be taken in a lot of the areas, due to the proliferation of ammunition and ordnance, which almost 60 years after the battle may be in a dangerous condition.

Atop Five Brothers stands a memorial to the 1st Marine Division and, inland of Beach Orange, stands the 81st Infantry Division monument, which was originally part of the Peleliu Military Cemetery, though the

The shell of this LVT(A)4 stands in silent testimony to the bloody battle that raged here in the fall of 1944. Although the jungle is rapidly doing its best to obliterate the scars, the visitor to the island can still stumble across numerous reminders of the struggle scattered here and there across the island. (Eric Mailander)

cemetery has long gone and is now overgrown by dense vegetation. Remains interred in the American Military Cemetery were transferred to Manila, Hawaii, or US locations, according to the wishes of the next of kin. A Japanese memorial stands in the civilian cemetery on Peleliu.

A field survey of Peleliu carried out by the Micronesian Archaeological Society team in 1981, reported that the Japanese blockhouse on Orange 3 that had held up the 3/7 remained "largely intact" and many other installations were located and charted. The full report, *Peleliu Revisited*, by D. Colt Denfeld, Micronesian Archaeological Survey Report #24, gives a fairly detailed account of the battle, followed by an in-depth survey report of the entirety of both Peleliu and Angaur, although the reader must note that the survey was done in 1988 and not all the relics survive today, but many do survive and more are unearthed each year.

The Palau islands are easily accessed, with regular flights from Guam to Koror. Most visitors stay on Koror or Arakabesang Islands, the majority of hotels being on Koror. Peleliu can be accessed from Koror by boat or plane. Occasionally, small groups of veterans and historians of the battle visit to reflect and remember, but these are growing fewer and fewer as the years go by, and soon nature will have covered any last remaining scars of a battle fought so bitterly many years ago.

BIBLIOGRAPHY

Denfield, D. Colt, *Peleliu Revisited: An Historical and Archaeological Survey of World War II Sites on Peleliu Island, Micronesian Archaeological Survey Report No. 24*, Saipan, The Micronesian Archaeological Survey, 1988

The 81st Wildcat Division Historical Committee, *The 81st Infantry Wildcat Division in World War II*, Washington, DC, Infantry Journal Press, 1948

Hallas, James, *The Devil's Anvil: The Assault on Peleliu*, Greenwood, CT: Praeger, 1994

Hough, Maj Frank O., *The Assault on Peleliu*, Historical Division, US Marine Corps: 1950 (Battery Press reprint available)

Gailey, Harry A., *Peleliu 1944*, Baltimore: Nautical & Aviation Company, 1983

Garand, George W. and Strobridge, Truman R., *History of US Marine Corps Operations in World War II: Western Pacific Operations, Vol. IV*, Washington, DC, US Government Printing Office, 1958

Gayle, BrigGen Gordon D., *Bloody Beaches: The Marines at Peleliu*, Washington Navy Yard, History and Museums Division, Marine Corps Historical Center, 1996

McMillian, George, *The Old Breed: A History of the First Marine Division in World War II*, Washington, DC, Infantry Journal Press, 1949 (Battery Press reprint available)

Moran, Jim, *US Marine Corps Uniforms and Equipment of World War II*, London, Windrow & Greene, 1992

Morison, Samuel E., *History of US Navy Operations in World War II: Leyte, June 1944–January 1944, Vol. XII*, Boston, Little, Brown & Company, 1966

Ross, Bill D., *Peleliu: Tragic Triumph, The Untold Story of the Pacific War's Forgotten Battle*, New York, Random House, 1992

Rottman, Gordon L., *World War II Pacific Island Guide: A Geo-Military Study*, Westport, CT, Greenwood Publishing, 2001.

Rottman, Gordon L., *US Marine Corps World War II Order of Battle: Ground and Air Units of the Pacific War, 1939–1945*, Westport, CT, Greenwood Publishing, 2001.

Sledge, Eugene B., With the Old Breed: At Peleliu and Okinawa, Novato, CA, Presidio, 1990

Stanton, Shelby L., US Army Uniforms of World War II, Harrisburg, PA, Stackpole Books, 1991

Smith, Robert R. United States Army in World War II: The Approach to the Philippines, Washington, DC: US Government Printing Office, 1984

INDEX

Nimitz, Admiral Chester William (1885–1966) 7, **7**, 8, **8**, 8–9, 16
Northern Pacific theatre of operations 7

Obata Hideyoshi, Lieutenant General 22
Oldendorf, Rear Admiral Jesse B. 18, 23, 29, 44, 77
Operation Stalemate **7**, 8, 16–17
Operation Stalemate II 8, 17–18, 20–21, 24, 29

Palau Islands, the 9, 9–10, **11**(map), 12–13
Pavuvu Island **15**, **20**, 29–30
Peleliu Island 12–13, 16, **19**(map), **59**(map), 92–93
Pennsylvania, USS 29
Philippines, the 7–9, 12
Point, The **35**, 49–51
Portland, USS 29
practice landings 40
pre-invasion bombardment **23**, 41, 44
   Angaur Island 68
prisoners of war 72, **89**, 89
pronunciation 13
Puller, Colonel Lewis B. "Chesty" **14**, 25, 65, 66, 91

Rabaul 7
railroad 13
reef, the 12
Romauldo Pocket, Angaur 70–71
Roosevelt, President Franklin Delano (1882–1945) **7**, 8
Rupertus, Major General William Henry (1889–1945) **12**, **16**, 21, 22, 24, 24–25, 40, 81, 82, 91
   and the assault on Ngesebus Island 77
   concerns 53
   on Peleliu 58, 63, 66
      and the Umurbrogol Pocket 83, 84–85

Sadao Inoue, Lieutenant General 9, 28
Saipan Island 16
Saipan Town 13, 69
Seawolf, USS 16
Selden, Colonel John T. 25
Shofner, Colonel Austin C. 51, 51–52
Short, Colonel James C. 26
significance 91
Smith, Lieutenant General Holland ("Howlin Mad") (1882–1967) 7
Smith, Major General Julian (1885–1975) 17, 23–24, 29
Smith, Brigadier General Oliver P. 25, 82
Smith, Major General Ralph Corbett 7
Solomon Islands 8
southeast promontory 60
southwest promontory 60–61
strategic situation 6, **6**(map)
submarine bases 12

temperature 59, 82
Tennessee, USS 29, 68
Terauchi Hisaichi, Field Marshal Count 22
terrain 12–13, 58–59, **61**, **64**
Tojo, Premier Hideki (1884–1948) 9, 27
Truk 7, 9, 10, 12, 21

Ulithi Atoll 17, 21, 33, 38, 70, 72

Umurbrogol Mountains, the 12–13, 21, 62, 63, 64–66, **83**(map), **85**
Umurbrogol Pocket, the **80**, 81–85, **84**, 88, **90**, 92
US forces
   1st Marine Division 7, 9, **15**, 17, **20**, 24–25, 29–30, 31–33, 33(table), 85
      1st Engineer Battalion 50
      1st Marines 20, 25, 26, 33, **35**, **39**, 45, 49–51, 53, 58, 62, 63–66, **68**, 73, 89
      1st Motor Transport Battalion 31
      1st Pioneer Battalion 33
      1st Reconnaissance Company 30
      1st Tank Battalion 30, 31, **56**, **77**, 82
      5th Marines 20, 26, 33, 51–52, 53, 57–58, 61–63, 73, 76–77, 82, 83–84, 89
      7th Marines 20, 25, 33, **41**, **48**, 51, 52–53, 58–59, 60–61, **66**, 73, 76, 77, 81, 82–83, 89
      11th Marines 20, 26, 31
      17th Marines 31
      Amphibian Tractor Battalions 30, 30–31
      Combat Teams 33
      US Navy Flamethrower Detachment 33, **80**, 82
   5th Marine Division 17
   27th Infantry Division 7
   31st Infantry Division 9
   77th Infantry Division 17
   81st Infantry Division 7, 9, 13, 17, 21, 26, 34(table), 34–35, 66–67, **84**, 89, 90–91
      321st Regimental Combat Team (RCT) 21, 26, 33–34, 66, 68, 69, 69–70, 71, 72, 73, 73(table), 76, 81, 85, 88, 90
      322nd Regimental Combat Team (RCT) 21, 26, 33–34, 68, 69, 70, 70–71, 88
      323rd Regimental Combat Team (RCT) 26, 33, 68, 85
      710th Tank Battalion 35
      casualties 71–72
   African Americans **36**, 53
   air support 8, 18, 62–63, 77, 85, 88, **90**
      on Angaur 68–72
   Angaur Landing Force 17
   artillery battalions 20–21, 31, 35
   casualties 9, **63**, 64, 66, 83, 89
      on Angaur 69, 71–72
      friendly fire 62–63, 69
      on Ulithi 72
   clear islands 85, 88
   command control 29
   confusion 51, 52–53
   DUKW amphibians **17**, 33, **40**
   Eastern Attack Force (TF33) 18
   Escort Carrier Group 18
   expectations 22
   III Amphibious Corps 16, 17, 24
   intelligence 12–13, 16–17, 39, 58–59
   inter-branch rivalry 7, 23, 25
   Kossol Passage Detachment 18
   landing vehicles, tracked (LVTs) **24**, **27**, 31, 33, **37**, 41, **48**, **65**, **76**, **93**
   medical services **48**
   the naval construction battalion ("the Seabees") 31, **44**, 73, 90, 91

on Ngesebus Island **76**, 77, **77**, 81
organization 18(table), 30, 31–33, 33(table), 34(table), 34–35
on Peleliu
   1st Marines replaced 73
   D+1 58–60, 61–62, 63–64
   D+2 60, 62, 64
   D+3 60–61, 62–63, 65
   D+4 63, 65–66
   D+5–6 63, 66
   D-Day **35**, **39**
   garrison 90–91
   intelligence gathering operations 16
   Japanese counter-attacks **56**, 57–58, 64
   landings **29**, **30**, **31**, **32**, 44–45, **48**, 49–53
   secure the north 76–77, 81
   and the Umurbrogol Pocket **80**, 81–85, **84**, 88, **90**
Peleliu Landing Force 17
plans 29, 41
   landings 18, 19–20
   pre-invasion bombardment **23**, 29, 41, 44
replacements **48**
and the Romauldo Pocket 70–71
strength 36
supplies **72**
tank dozers **69**
tanks 30, 31, 35, 49, 52–53, **53**, **56**, 60, **77**, 81, 82
Third Fleet 17–18
on Ulithi Atoll 72
Underwater Demolition Teams (UDTs) 40–41
war dogs **62**
water supplies 59–60, **60**
weapons 32–33, 35, **70**, **80**, **82**
Western Attack Force (TF32) 17–18
Western Fire Support Group 18
Western Landing Force 17
Western Task Force 29
X-Ray Provisional Amphibious Corps 17
XXIV Corps 16, 17
Ushio Goto, Major 39

Venable, Colonel Benjamin W. 26

Walt, Lieutenant Colonel Lewis W. 52, 61–62, 77
Wasp, USS 68
Watson, Colonel Arthur P. 26, 88
weapons
   bazookas 32, **70**, **80**
      flamethrowers 32, 37, **80**, **82**
      M1 carbine 32–33
      M1 rifle 35
      machine guns 32, 35, 36, 37
      mortars 32, 35, 37, 38, **80**
weather 82
West Road, the 73, 76
Wildcat Bowl 88
Wilkinson, Vice Admiral Theodore S. 18, 23, 85
Willis, Lieutenant William L. 50

Yamaguchi Takso, Major General 10, 21, 37–38
Yap 12, 16, 17, 38